Chosen for Destruction:

The Story of a Holocaust Survivor

During the years when I should have proudly walked the streets of my hometown wearing the insignia of my school, I instead wore the Star of David or a yellow stripe in Nazi ghettos and camps to signify that I was a Jew chosen for destruction.

Morris Glass

Morris Glass
and
Carolyn Murray Happer

Contents

To
My dear wife, Carol,
and to
my family
who perished in the Holocaust.

Morris Glass

To
My parents,
Carolyn and Bill Murray.

Carolyn Murray Happer

Acknowledgements

In writing this book, I have been assisted by many people. Of foremost importance is Morris Glass, who spent countless hours relating his story and elaborating the details so that I could understand his life during the Holocaust. I am grateful for his willingness to explore and share his memories of a painful time. He was patient with me, and I learned much from our conversations. I also thank his wife, Carol, who was unfailingly hospitable and supportive.

The staff in the library at Meredith College was crucial in helping me find resources there and elsewhere, and in furnishing me equipment and teaching me how to use it. I particularly thank Rick McBane and John Kincheloe in Media Services, Dianne Andrews in Interlibrary Loans, and Judy Schuster, a reference librarian. I also thank Robin Baneth, in Technology Services, for helping me to master various computer programs.

My colleagues in the History and Political Science Department willingly read the manuscript, advised, and encouraged me. In this regard, I recognize Daniel Fountain, Clyde Frazier, Jeffrey Martinson, Michael Novak, Hilary Smith, Barbara True-Weber, and Gregory Vitarbo. When in doubt about grammar, I was advised by Diana Davis, our departmental assistant, and by Robin Colby, a colleague in the Department of English. Two students offered valuable assistance: Brittany Wuester, who spent hours transcribing my taped conversations with Morris, and Amber Horton, who proofread the final draft.

I express special thanks to Elizabeth Crowder for editing the final draft. She is knowledgeable, meticulous, and patient. I learned much from her corrections and advice.

Finally, I thank the members of my family and the many friends who helped me by reading the manuscript and by enthusiastically supporting this project. I especially thank my son, Marshall Happer, who helped with the many German words and phrases in the book; my niece, Betty Witman, who assisted me with the publication; my Kirby cousins, who provided a quiet place to write, and, above all, my sister Cissie Donigan (now deceased), who read the manuscript, offered advice, and inspired me in many ways. I am also indebted to Michael Lanning, who was an endless source of support; Janice Swab and Danny Green, who read the final draft; and William Price and Nan Miller, both of whom advised and encouraged me.

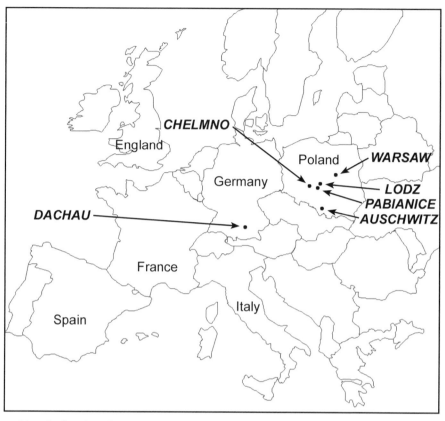

Map indicating the places where Morris was located. (The present-day
map of Europe is used because the boundaries in Europe, during the time
Morris lived there, were constantly changing.)

Introduction

I am a Jew from Poland and therein lies a tale of proscription, persecution, and loss. Anti-Semitism, ghettos, selections, deportations, and concentration camps formed the context of my youth. While my experiences and that of my family were unique, they also reflect the experiences of countless other victims of the Nazi regime. In this book I hope that I can tell not only my story but that I can also illuminate what happened to millions of other Jews who were caught in a maelstrom beyond their control. Morris Glass

Morris Glass was eleven years old when the Nazis invaded Poland and changed his life forever. Suddenly a childhood filled with school, soccer, and cowboy movies was transformed into a nightmare of exhausting work, hunger, cold, fear, and loss. Morris spent four and a half years in Polish ghettos, two months in Auschwitz-Birkenau, and seven months in various work camps that were part of the Dachau system. At the end of the war, he was liberated by the American army. During these years, he lost his youth, his home, and his father, mother, and two sisters. Out of forty-two close family members, only Morris, his brother, and a first cousin survived.

Since 1949, Morris has been proud to live in the United States—as he says, "I owe my life to the American army." During most of his adult life, Morris lived in New Jersey where he was the owner of a successful clothing company and where he married and became the father of four boys and three girls. Presently, he is retired and living in Raleigh, North Carolina. At the time of this writing, Morris is in his early eighties. He has grey hair and light brown eyes and is always smartly and immaculately dressed. His perfect posture gives the impression that he is much larger than he actually is. A cheerful demeanor, an optimistic attitude, and an enthusiasm for life make Morris a compelling personality and his obvious leadership qualities command respect and attention. Considering all that Morris has endured and witnessed, he is amazingly free of anger and bitterness. While aware of the frailties of humans, he is forgiving, positive, and inclusive.

My path first crossed with Morris in the spring of 2007, when I heard him speak at the North Carolina Holocaust Commemoration service which was held at Meredith College where I teach history. I was mesmerized by his retelling of his experiences during the Holocaust. His story was riveting—no one moved during the half hour that he spoke. His narrative was so compelling and he was so charismatic that I said to myself, "His is a story that needs to reach a wider audience." Not long afterward I asked Morris if he would be interested in my writing about his experiences. To my delight, he agreed. That was the beginning of a partnership and a friendship which has encompassed some two years of conversations, research, and writing.

The result of our collaboration is a narrative that interweaves Morris's recollections with my explanation of the huge, impersonal forces that had a very personal impact on him and millions of other ordinary humans who happened to be Jewish. There are survivors' accounts that allude to the larger events into which people were swept, and there are histories which illustrate broad developments with examples from survivors' testimonies. But as far as I know, there is no book that attempts to be both a history and an autobiography. It is the mix of memoir and history that makes this narrative unique.

Although much has been written about those who survived the Holocaust, Morris's story is worth telling for a number of reasons: first, the long extent of time that he was subjected to Nazi rule; second, the variety of his experiences during the Holocaust, and third, the need to emphasize the enormity of the annihilation of the Polish Jews.

For over five and a half years, Morris was a victim of the Nazi regime. He was living in western Poland when it was conquered in September, 1939, and he was an inmate in a concentration camp in Germany until the final days of the war in the spring of 1945. Not only was he under the control of the Nazis for a very long time, but he was also confined in the longest-lasting ghetto, a situation which may partially account for his survival. Few Jews, whether from Poland or elsewhere, survived in captivity as long as he.

While it is difficult to generalize about the Jewish experience under the Nazis, Morris's story does encompass large aspects of it. He watched as the conquering German army marched through his town and he witnessed the subsequent burning of books and the main synagogue there; he experienced life in two ghettos, deportation on the death trains, selection at Auschwitz-Birkenau, and confinement as a slave laborer in a number of work camps. The one major aspect of the Holocaust that was not a part of his experience was the open-air shooting of Jews which followed the German invasion of the Soviet Union in 1941. This rampage of killing resulted in the murder of approximately one and a half million Jews.

The final justification for yet another book on the Jewish Holocaust is to add more weight to the experience of the Polish Jews. Of the victims of the annihilation, fully half were Polish and in no area was the annihilation more complete. Nevertheless, for a number of reasons the preponderance of survivor accounts has tended to describe the experience of Hungarian and western European Jews. *The Diary of Anne Frank* by a girl from Amsterdam; *Night* by Elie Wiesel, a boy from what was then Hungary, and *Survival at Auschwitz* by the Italian Primo Levi are arguably the most widely read accounts by Holocaust survivors, but, even though Wiesel and Levi describe the time that they spent in Poland, none of these books touches on the experience of the Polish Jews.

The combination of autobiography and historical description has dictated the way the narrative is organized. It is written in two voices: Morris's, that of a survivor, and mine, that of an historian. Different fonts indicate which of us is speaking; the autobiography is in italics and the history is in roman type. The opening chapter belongs entirely to me as I recount the developments that came together in the twentieth century to make possible the genocide of the European Jews. Most of the remaining chapters intersperse my explanatory information with Morris's story. For example, I describe and account for Jewish ghettos in the chapter where Morris is forced into his hometown ghetto. Sometimes the voice of the historian is dominant, most notably in the chapter which describes and accounts for the longevity of the Lodz ghetto. In other chapters, especially the one which describes the seven months that Morris was imprisoned in the Dachau camps, the narrative is almost exclusively Morris's. Most chapters are introduced by a quotation from Morris.

Morris's recollections, comprising over fifty hours of interviews, are the main source for this book. Most of the interviews were conducted in the fall of 2008; but Morris added some additional material in later conversations with me. Morris is, as he says, "blessed with a tremendous memory and an ability to recall" things that happened a very long time ago. His memory, as corroborated by other accounts of the same events and circumstances, is quite accurate.

The distance between the actual events and Morris's retelling of them does, however, place limitations on his recollections. His life during these years consisted of an endless repetition of a colorless routine; unless something unusual occurred, the ordinariness of his life melded one day into the next. Morris's memory of crises or dramatic turning points like his arrival and selection at Auschwitz encompasses details about the weather, the arrival and processing time, what he wore, how he felt, and what he or others said. But without something out of the ordinary, he has few knobs on which to hang his memories.

In addition to his distance from events, Morris's account is shaped, probably unconsciously, by an adherence to a path that he has followed while venturing into his past. When listening to him talk, one senses a reluctance to wander out of the safety of this well trodden path. For example, the time that I observed Morris having the most difficulty coping with his remembrances occurred when we were talking about the Lodz ghetto. I was pressing him to describe what he did when he was not working and something we were talking about triggered him to recall Mala, his "sweetheart" in the ghetto. He said that this was the first time that he had thought of her since he was a boy. The memory was obviously painful.

Morris did not avoid talking about the horror and cruelty that he experienced and witnessed. Even though the description of some events, such as the last time he saw his mother and sisters on the railroad platform at Auschwitz and the death of his father, still have the power to elicit fresh and raw emotions, he remained candid. But neither did he exaggerate his suffering or that of other Jews. Several times he referred to his loathing of distorted and sensationalized accounts of Nazi atrocities—"The Nazis were so bad and their acts so evil, that there is no need to embellish them."

One problem I had in listening to Morris's narrative was that of separating his past remembrances from information that he had subsequently acquired. Morris is extraordinarily knowledgeable about the history of the Holocaust and World War II, and in our conversations he often and easily shifted back and forth between what he had experienced and knew at the time and what he had learned later. I had to be very careful to distinguish between the two. As the interviews progressed, he made my task easier by stating something like, "As I later learned." I never heard him make an error; he knows his history.

As to my explanation of the developments that led to and occurred during the Holocaust, I have relied on numerous sources. In addition to the general histories of the Holocaust, I was careful to examine the more specific histories of the Lodz ghetto and of the Dachau camps. I also searched for testimonies by survivors whose experiences were similar to Morris's. Among these I found testimonies by Jack Adler and Helen Chmura Aronson, two people from Morris's hometown. I also found a brief account by Morris's brother Nachman. I have had the privilege of meeting and listening to a number of survivors whose stories gave me further insight into Morris's experiences. I have also watched numerous documentaries, especially those about Poland: *Lodz Ghetto, Shtetl, and Shoah* were especially helpful. I found a number of excellent web sites; the United States Holocaust Memorial Museum's web site (ushmm.org) and a site devoted to the Kaufering camps (kaufering.com) were especially helpful. When in doubt as to a statistic, date, person, etc., I relied on *The Destruction of the European Jews* by Raul Hilberg and the *Holocaust Encyclopedia.*

In recounting his experiences, Morris uses words and phrases from Polish, German, and Hebrew. I have italicized these words and, the first time that they are used, I have included a translation within brackets. Also, when talking about his family, friends, and acquaintances during his childhood and the Holocaust, Morris refers to them using the Polish pronunciation; I have followed his lead. The one exception to this is Morris himself. Although *Moniek* is Morris's Polish name, throughout the book I have referred to him as "Morris."

My association with Morris has enriched my life enormously; it has opened up insights into the human psyche that have both pained and inspired me. I am indeed grateful that I have had the opportunity to know him and that he has been willing to share his past with me and others. It is my hope that this book will both throw light on one boy's experiences and illuminate one of history's darkest chapters.

Chapter 2

Historical Background to the Holocaust

I was born in Pabianice, Poland, on April 3, 1928. Eleven years later, on September 1, 1939, the German army with all of its armor and motorized vehicles marched into Poland and changed my life forever. The next six years were absolute hell for me and the Jews of Poland. Never could we have imagined the destruction and death that this day would unleash. For me these years would mean hunger and fear on a scale I simply have not the words to describe; they would mean the destruction of all of my close relatives, except my brother and a first cousin, and they would mean the death of some six million Jews. Morris Glass

The destruction of Morris's family and the other victims of the Nazis did not occur in a vacuum. Rather, it occurred in a field that had been well prepared by millennia of Christian anti-Semitism and its more recent secular mutant, racial anti-Semitism, and by the disillusionment with Western values and institutions that had occurred in Germany and elsewhere in Europe as a consequence of the destruction and futility of World War I. Persecution of the Jews was not new to the West. What was new to the Holocaust was the Nazis' goal of destroying all of the Jews in Europe, a goal that they euphemistically called the Final Solution, and their use of science and industrial technology to accomplish this mass murder.

The events that ultimately led to the Holocaust were set in motion some two thousand years ago when the Romans expelled the Jews from Palestine following a revolt against the Empire. Thus began the *Diaspora,*

the long dispersion of the Jews throughout the world. Some of the exiled Jews settled in western Europe where for a millennium they lived in
uneasy harmony with Christians in a civilization that was by definition
Christian, whose boundaries were the same as the Roman Catholic Church,
and in which the most powerful and richest institution was the Church.
For various reasons, one of which was the goal of converting the Jews to
Christianity, the Jews were the only non-Christians who were permitted to
dwell in what was then called Christendom. Living within a religious community which considered them to have been responsible for the death of
its God was perilous indeed for the Jews. The accusation of "Christ killer"
began early and it continued to permeate the thinking of many Christians
down through the centuries; it is a term with which Morris is very familiar.
It was not until after the Holocaust that the Roman Catholic Church and the
major Protestant denominations moved toward repudiating this concept and
apologizing for the tradition of Christian anti-Semitism.[1]

The fragile peace between Jews and Christians ended in the late
1000s with the advent of the Crusades. Ironically, these campaigns, which
originated as an effort to drive the Muslim infidels from the Holy Land,
inflamed feelings against the Jewish infidels in Europe. The heightened
emotions against the Jews in turn ignited massive violence against them.
Thus, as the Christian armies moved through Europe on their way to
Palestine, they began slaughtering the Jewish non-believers in their midst.
The slaughter was especially intense along the Rhine River, one of the
main routes used by the Crusaders.

The Crusades were followed in the mid-1300s by the Great Plague
which killed approximately one-third of the population of Europe—it was
the worst disaster ever to visit Western civilization. No one at the time
understood the cause of this catastrophe and terror gripped the population.
Despite the fact that they were also dying, the Jews were blamed for the
plague and consequently punished in horrible ways. Because the punish-
ments were so terrible, a crime had to be manufactured to justify them.
Thus was born the fiction of the "blood libel," also called "ritual murder,"
which alleges that Jews kidnap Christian children and use their blood to
make the food for the Jewish Holy Days. Other crimes were invented but
the allegation of ritual murder was the most persistent and damaging. Hard
as it is to believe, a little over a year after the end of World War II in July,
1946, forty-two Jews were murdered in a pogrom in Kelice, Poland that
was fueled by rumors of the kidnapping of a Christian child.[2]

The Plague was followed in the early 1500s by the Reformation, a quarrel among Western Christians about how one is saved. This intensely religious conflict, which ultimately split Western Christianity into Protestant and Roman Catholic, aggravated animosity towards the Jews instead of lessening it. The leader of the Protestants, Martin Luther, infuriated because the Jews had failed to convert to his new brand of Christianity, lashed out at them labeling them, "miserable, wicked people, …liars and bloodhounds, …boastful, proud fools, …bloodthirsty and revengeful, …a plague, pestilence, and nothing but a misfortune." He urged that Christians take a number of actions against the Jews including that "we refuse them the right to have synagogues," that "we take away from them all their prayer books and Talmunds," and that [if the rulers do not restrain them] "they be driven from the country …and be told to move to their own land and possessions in Jerusalem and there lie, curse, blaspheme, spit, murder, steal, rob, practice usury, mock and engage in all such slanderous abominations." [3] Nowhere was Luther's legacy more pervasive and enduring than in Germany.

The animosity aroused by the Crusades, the Great Plague, and the Reformation led not only to the persecution of many Jews but also, mainly in the fourteenth and fifteenth centuries, to their expulsion from most of the countries of western Europe. Some of the exiled Jews went to northern Africa and some went to eastern Europe where they became concentrated in an area stretching from the Baltic to the Black Sea. This area, which came to be known as the Pale, included present-day Latvia, Lithuania, Poland, Belarus, Moldova and Ukraine.[4] Here, the Jews were generally welcomed as laborers, and they lived in relative harmony with their Slavic neighbors until the mid-1600s when they became the scapegoat for ethnic conflicts in the area. The worst atrocity committed against them before the Holocaust, the Chmielnicki Massacres, occurred in Ukraine between 1648 and 1658, when the Cossacks murdered hundreds of thousands of Jews in horrible ways. Although slaughter on this scale was not repeated until the Holocaust, life was increasingly difficult for Jews in the Pale. As a result some migrated back into western Europe.

When Russian nationalism emerged in the last decades of the 1800s, the situation of the Jews in the Pale turned from unpleasant to perilous. As efforts were made to promote a consciousness among Russians that they constituted a unique national group, the Jews were increasingly seen as outsiders, a people who were different and who were definitely not Russian. The resulting surge of anti-Semitism was accompanied by numerous and brutal pogroms. This violence against the Jews led, in the decades immediately preceding and following 1900, to the emigration of approximately two million eastern Jews, primarily to the United States.

Paradoxically, another consequence of this escalating anti-Semitism was to arouse feelings of Jewish nationalism which in turn led to the birth of Zionism, the drive to establish a Jewish state. The person most responsible for shaping and giving substance to Zionism was Theodor Herzl, a Viennese Jew whose vision of a Jewish state inspired the creation of Zionist groups and also encouraged immigration to Palestine.

Meanwhile in western Europe in the late eighteenth and nineteenth centuries, those Jews who had remained there or who had returned were enjoying a new atmosphere of toleration and equality stemming from the Enlightenment concept of natural rights. As a result many Jews in the countries of Western Europe began to assimilate and excel. Marx, Freud, Einstein, and the Rothschilds are examples of Jews who became prominent in the late nineteenth and early twentieth centuries. Unfortunately, the success of Jews, especially in business, bred jealousy and resentment among some Gentiles. Ironically, while the opportunity to assimilate into the mainstream of western European life offered Jews security from oppression and the possibility of advancement, it also posed a threat to their historic uniqueness and identity.

At the same time that the Jews in western Europe were entering into the mainstream of political, economic, and social life, a new form of secular anti-Semitism, known as Social Darwinism, was being articulated. This new racially based anti-Semitism was grounded in pseudoscientific ideas stemming from a distorted interpretation of Darwin's theory of evolution through natural selection. According to racial or biological anti-Semitism, the Germanic/Aryan peoples had triumphed in the struggle for survival and therefore constituted the highest form of humans. On the other hand Jews, Slavs, and blacks were among the inferior races, the losers in this struggle. It followed that the continued existence of Jews lowered the level of civilization. Furthermore, the possibility of Jews breeding with the superior race, posed a threat to its racial purity. While religious anti-Semitism had offered Jews an escape clause—conversion, there was no escape from biology. The logical conclusion of race-based anti-Semitism was that inferior peoples should be eliminated. Trumpeted as backed by science, this new form of anti-Semitism was a good fit for the scientific, industrial, and increasingly secular countries of western Europe. However, in eastern Europe, where the modern world had barely penetrated, it appears that the dominant expression of anti-Semitism continued to be based on religion.[5]

In contrast to the surge of violence against the Jews in eastern Europe in the late nineteenth century, anti-Semitism appeared to be waning in the West. The new racial anti-Semitism seemingly had little mass appeal and it remained confined to fringe groups. Unfortunately in the twentieth century, the Nazis, who originated as a small political party on the extreme right, seized upon racial anti-Semitism and used it to gain power in Germany and then to justify their attempt to annihilate the Jews and other peoples they deemed inferior. Nevertheless, at the turn of the century, despite the birth of racial anti-Semitism and incidents like the Dreyfus trial in France, anti-Semitism in the West, appeared to be a dying phenomenon.[6]

But then came World War I (1914-1918), four years of unprecedented slaughter, that left Europeans exhausted, disillusioned, and bitter. No country was more devastated than Germany. Not only did she suffer enormous casualties on the front and terrible shortages at home but she also lost the war. Defeat was followed by a harsh treaty that imposed huge reparations on Germany, took away German lands, and limited the German military to a small defensive force. As a result, Germany's new, democratic government, the Weimar Republic, was handicapped from the beginning. Its chance of success was further diminished in 1923 by an inflation that totally destroyed the monetary system and financially ruined many people, especially those in the middle class.

Just as Germany seemed to be returning to stability and prosperity, the Great Depression hit and by 1932 approximately one-third of German workers were unemployed. This economic crisis produced a political one that vaulted Hitler to power in January 1933. Once in power Hitler moved quickly to concentrate all power in his hands, and by April of 1933, Germany was a dictatorship under a *Führer* [Leader] who was dedicated to achieving German greatness. The means to this end would be the creation of a Master Race of pure Germans which in turn would mean the elimination of those who were polluting German blood, notably the Jews.

Over the next several years, the Jews in Germany were removed from professions, schools, and public life, stripped of their citizenship, forbidden to intermarry, and subjected to personal insults; in addition, their property and wealth were confiscated. In 1938, the Nazis expelled all Polish-born Jews from Germany; among them were Morris's great-uncle Bernard and his son Max. However, until *Kristallnacht* [Crystal Night], November 9-10, 1938, personal violence against the Jews in Germany was limited—but on that night, the Nazis went on a rampage. They smashed the windows of Jewish merchants and looted their businesses, burned synagogues, ransacked Jewish homes, harassed and killed Jews, and arrested thousands of Jewish men and sent them to Dachau and other places. The violence of *Kristallnacht* ended any illusions about the Nazis' intentions and made it very clear to Jews and Gentiles alike that the Nazis planned to make Germany free of Jews.

Before *Kristallnacht* but increasingly afterwards, emigration was the goal of most German Jews. Unfortunately, their desire to leave Germany was frustrated by the formidable barriers to immigration erected by governments like that of the United States. As a result, when World War II began in 1939 and immigration became impossible, slightly over half of Germany's Jews had been able to leave. The rest were trapped, and most were later murdered.[7] While the German Jews had at least had a limited opportunity to leave, the Jews in the countries that Germany occupied after World War II began had virtually no possibility to leave. Some Jews in Poland, like Morris's first cousin, did escape by fleeing deep into the Soviet Union, but they were the exception.

The beginning of World War II in September, 1939, did not inaugurate the genocide. Although life was increasingly perilous for the Jews under Nazi control, the decision to annihilate them had not yet been made. In fact, as late as 1941 the Nazis were still talking about solving the Jewish problem by resettling them on the French-held island of Madagascar. Even in Poland, the Nazis focused on murdering the Polish elites—the political, religious, and military leaders, the professional classes, and the intellectuals—and not the Jews. All of this was to change in June 1941, when Germany invaded the Soviet Union.

The decision to attack the Soviet Union reversed the original German strategy which was to fight only on one front. Hitler, who had been a soldier in the First World War, understood well the dangers of a two-front war and thus he assiduously tried to avoid a war in the East until he had defeated the western countries. To secure this result, in 1939 before Germany invaded Poland, Hitler had signed a nonaggression treaty with Stalin. By this treaty both countries publicly agreed not to attack each other; privately, they agreed to invade Poland and to divide her between them. Shortly after signing this treaty, Germany and, a few weeks later, the Soviet Union invaded, defeated, and partitioned Poland; afterward, Germany took control over the western half of Poland, the area where Morris lived. Hitler then turned his attention toward western Europe, which he invaded in the spring of 1940. When it became clear by the fall of 1940 that an invasion of Britain and thus total victory in the West was impossible, Hitler began, despite his treaty obligations, to plan for an invasion of the Soviet Union. The invasion which began on June 22, 1941, inaugurated a two-front war that would ultimately lead to the defeat of Germany. It also sounded the death knell for the Jews of Europe.

The invasion of the Soviet Union gave the Nazis access to the huge concentration of Jews in eastern Europe and, under the cover of war, the annihilation began. Following in the rear of the advancing German army, the *Wehrmacht* [literally "war machine"], were SS death squads, *Einsatzgruppen* [Special Action Squads], that rounded up Jews and shot them.[8] By the time the Nazi officials met at Wannsee, a suburb of Berlin in early 1942 and confirmed the Final Solution as official policy, it is estimated that close to a million Jews had already been murdered by the Einsatzgruppen.[9] Included in this number were some 33,000 Jews who were shot at Babi Yar, a ravine on the outskirts of Kiev, Ukraine, during a three-day operation in late September, 1941. The story of the shooting of the Jews in the Soviet Union is almost unknown in the West. The Cold War prevented access to these areas, and Stalin's hatred of the Jews made him refuse to recognize the uniqueness of their experience and to disengage it from the experiences of the Soviet people generally.

Shooting such a large number of people, however, proved to be messy and difficult for the perpetrators as well as inefficient, expensive, and too public. The solution to these problems was resolved by building centers for mass murder and then transporting the victims to the centers. The resulting six death camps were designed simply to kill a multitude of people as efficiently as possible by using gas, either carbon monoxide or Zyclon B. Primarily because of Poland's proximity to the huge concentrations of eastern European Jews, all of the killing centers were located there. With the establishment of the death camps, it is estimated that over two and a half million Jews were murdered in 1942, the peak year for deaths. In 1943, the total dropped to about half a million. In 1944 there was a slight increase in the murders primarily because of the annihilation of the Hungarian Jews.[10] While Jews constituted the overwhelming number of victims of the Nazi death industry, they were not the only victims. Also included among those murdered were Polish Gentiles and other Slavic peoples, Russian POWs, gypsies, Communists and Socialists, Jehovah's Witnesses, and homosexuals.

In addition to the death camps and trains, the Final Solution also encompassed the establishment of ghettos and slave labor camps. In establishing Jewish ghettos the Nazis were reviving an old European tradition by which Jews were confined to a designated area. Some of the ghettos were used simply as holding pens where Jews were assembled before being transported to their death. Others, like Lodz where Morris and his family were held, also functioned as centers for manufacturing armaments, uniforms, and other products essential for the Nazi war effort; this work, however, simply postponed the workers' inevitable deportation and death. The Nazis also built camps where the prisoners produced materials for the war. Many hundreds of these camps were located throughout Germany and the occupied areas. Here the inmates were literally worked to death by doing hard labor in unspeakable conditions. Although these were not death camps, they accomplished much the same purpose albeit at a slower pace. Morris was an inmate in five camps that were satellites of Dachau, one of the most infamous of these camps.

The annihilation by bullets, gas, work, and starvation did not end until the Allies converged on Germany in the last months of the war. Because the Soviets advanced from the east through Poland, they liberated what was left of the death camps; however, many of the work camps in Germany were liberated by the British and Americans—Morris, who was in a work camp in southern Germany, was liberated by the Americans.

Following liberation, the survivors desperately searched for family members. Some returned to Poland where they were greeted with such hostility that most quickly left. Morris, and I suspect that his feelings were fairly typical of many other survivors, simply wanted to get out of Europe. In 1949, he and his brother immigrated to the United States.

In the aftermath of the fighting, some of those responsible for the murder escaped to other countries or adopted new identities. Others were caught, tried, and convicted; some were hanged and others were imprisoned. At this writing, the search for Nazi criminals continues.

Like most survivors, Morris had lost everything— family and friends, home, possessions and, in his case, his youth. As he states, *"During the years when I should have proudly walked the streets of my hometown wearing the insignia of my school, I instead wore the Star of David or a yellow stripe in the ghettos and camps to signify that I was a Jew chosen for destruction."* But, as he also states, *"I was lucky. I survived and found a new life in a new country. I count myself very fortunate."*

1. Perhaps the best-known example of Christian efforts toward reconciliation oc-
    curred under the leadership of Pope John XXIII and Pope Paul VI during the
    Second Vatican Council (1962-1965) when the Roman Catholic Church sought
    to distance itself from the belief in the collective responsibility of the Jews for

the death of Christ. In an official declaration, *Nostra Aetate [In Our Time]* the Council stated that although some Jews did demand the death of Jesus, the blame for his death cannot be placed on all of the Jews at the time or on subsequent generations of Jews.

Reconciliation of Catholics and Jews was further strengthened under Pope John Paul II (1920-2005) who established full diplomatic ties with Israel, visited Israel, and publicly apologized for the persecution of the Jews throughout history.

It should be noted that the Roman Catholic Church was by no means alone in its failure to denounce anti-Semitism and the Nazis or to respond to the plight of the Jews during the Holocaust. The only Christian denomination that openly opposed the Nazis was the Jehovah's Witnesses and they paid for their opposition with their lives. The estimates as to how many died in the camps or were executed varies; the *Holocaust Encyclopedia* estimates the figure at around two thousand. USHMM, "Jehovah's Witnesses," *Holocaust Encyclopedia*, http://www.ushmm.org/wlc/en/article.php?ModuleId=10005394 (accessed September 14, 2010).

2. A pogrom is organized violence that is often officially sanctioned and that is directed against a minority, especially Jews.

3. Martin Luther, *The Jews and Their Lies* (Los Angeles, CA: Christian Nationalist Crusade, 1948), 8, 14, 16, 17, 56, 41, 52.

4. Crowe, David M. "The Holocaust, Roots, History, and Aftermath (Boulder, CO: Westview Press, 2008), 31. "The impact of the forced expulsions in Spain, Portugal, and other parts of Western and Central Europe was dramatic. The estimated Jewish population of Europe in 1490 was 600,000, with 570,000 (95%) living in Western and Central Europe. Two centuries later, Europe's Jewish population, which numbered 716,000 in 1700, had shifted eastward. Only 20% of Europe's Jews now lived in the West; the rest were in Eastern Europe and the Balkans."

5. Jan T. Gross, *Neighbors* (Princeton, NJ: Princeton University Press, 2002), in particular the chapters "The Outbreak of the Russo-German War and the Pogrom in Radzilow," 30-42 and "Anachronism," 79-81. For examples of Christian anti-Semitism, see Claude Lanzmann, *Shoah*, VHS (New Yorker Films, 1985), tape 2.

6. Alfred Dreyfus, a Jew who was a captain in French army, was falsely accused of treason, tried and sentenced to prison where he remained until he was exonerated some twelve years later. His case was driven by anti-Semitism, and his trial (1894), which exposed the latent anti-Semitism in France, was undoubtedly the most famous trial in nineteenth-century Europe.

7. In 1933 there were approximately 523,000 Jews in Germany; by September, 1939 when World War II began, approximately 282,000 had emigrated; by the end of 1939 there were approximately 202,000 Jews remaining in Germany. USHMM, "German Jewish Refugees, 1933-1939," *Holocaust Encyclopedia*, http://www.ushmm.org/wlc/en/article.php?ModuleId=10005468 (accessed on September 17, 2010).

8. SS is the abbreviation for *Schutzstaffel* [Protection Squad]. Also known as the Blackshirts because of the color of their uniforms, the SS functioned as an elite military organization within the Nazi Party. It was separate from the *Wehrmacht* [the regular German army], and it swore its oath of loyalty directly to Hitler. There were several branches of the SS; among these were the Panzer [tank] divisions, the *Einsatzgruppen*, and the *Totenkopfverbände* [Death Groups], the administrators and guards of the concentration camps. All three groups wore the "death's head" on their caps. Heinrich Himmler was head of all of the divisions of the SS.

9. Raul Hilberg, *The Destruction of the European Jews*, 3rd ed., 3 vols (New Haven, CT: Yale University Press, 2003), 3:1320, Table B-1, *Deaths by Cause*. This table shows the causes of death as follows:

Ghettoization and general privation 800,000
Open-air shootings.. 1,400,000
Camps
    Death Camps.. 2,600,000
    Concentration, Labor and Transit Camps........................... 150,000
    Other Camps 150,000

10. Hilberg, *Destruction*, 3:1321, p. 1321, Table B-3, Deaths By Year. This table shows the death by years as follows:

1933-1940	under 100,000
1941	1,100,000
1942	**2,600,000**
1943	600,000
1944	600,000
1945	over 100,000
Total	5,100,000

Chapter 3

My Home and Family

I was born in the town of Pabianice, Poland on April 3, 1928, to a
prosperous Jewish family that included my parents, Yechiel and Esthera,
two sisters, Rozka and Bluma, and one brother, Nachman; I was the baby
of the family. Our family was close knit and I was well loved. In addition
to my immediate family I was surrounded by a host of relatives. Out of the
forty-two aunts, uncles, and first and second cousins who were living in
Poland when the war began in 1939, only three survived—a first cousin,
my brother, and I. Ours was a family living in the shadow of the Fall.
Morris Glass

My parents' family names, Glass and Kupperwasser, are German, and
although I do not know for certain, I suspect that both families were part
of an early migration of Jews from Germany. This is certainly a possibility
since my home town, Pabianice, is located in an area of western Poland
which has been linked to Germany by both proximity and history.[1] In fact,
for over a century, from 1795 to 1919, during which time Poland ceased to
exist, much of western Poland, including Pabianice, was under the control
of Prussia and then Germany. Although the boundary between Germany
and Poland was moved westward after World War II, at the time of the
invasion in 1939, Pabianice was only about fifty miles from Germany and a
number of Germans lived there—I don't know how many or what percent of
the population but their presence was noticeable.
  My family was connected in various ways to the neighboring city of
Lodz, the second-largest city in Poland. Located about fifteen miles to the

south of Pabianice, Lodz was a textile manufacturing center and for this reason it was called the "Manchester of Poland." Since my father was in the textile business, he was often in Lodz; my siblings went to high school there, and we had relatives who lived there. It was a city that played a large part in our lives both before and after the German invasion.

Home was an apartment that was located one block off the main street of Pabianice, Warsaw Street, in what was called the "Old City." It was down Warsaw Street that the trolley from Pabianice to Lodz ran, that the German army marched during its conquest of Poland in 1939, and that the Jews of Pabianice were forced to trudge when the town was made Judenfrei [Free of Jews] *in 1942. Most of the Jews of Pabianice lived in the Old City and consequently it was home to a number of synagogues, the largest of which was located within a block of our apartment. We could easily see it burning when the Nazis torched it after taking over the town.*

Our family lived in a beautiful, large, modern apartment with four bedrooms, a big living room, a dining room, and a huge kitchen. What made our apartment modern and luxurious was that it had a bathroom with a flush toilet and a tub where we bathed every Thursday evening in preparation for the Sabbath. Having such a bathroom was unusual for the time, especially in the Old City, where I would estimate that about 95 percent of the households still depended on outhouses. I doubt that any of my friends, except my best friend Abraham whose family had an apartment across the hall from ours, had ever even seen an indoor toilet and tub. Although our bathroom was modern by Old City standards, we still had to heat the water for our baths on a stove next to the tub. In addition to the toilet and tub, we also had a telephone. Having all of these conveniences practically made us royalty! I can still remember our phone number, 110, and my father's business number, 20. That these numbers were so low indicates just how rare telephones were in prewar Poland.

Behind our apartment building was a large yard where the children played and where each family had a shed where they could store coal and tools. There was also a water pump in the yard that was used to wash clothes and linens. The laundry was then hung in an attic shared by the eight families who lived in the building. My family employed a woman who came every week or so to wash for us.

Our apartment was the center of my family's life, and my family was the center of my early years. As with most children, almost all of my earliest remembrances revolve around family. In 1939 when the war began, my father and mother were both in their early forties. My oldest sister was

19; my brother was 17, and my younger sister was 15. I was only 11 but during most of the Holocaust I pretended to be a year older than I was— at Dachau my birth year is recorded as 1927 instead of the correct date of 1928. Our family was indeed fortunate because all of us were of an age to work for the Germans. Since the first Jews to be murdered were usually those who were either too old or too young to work, being of working age partially explains why each of us survived as long as we did.

Amazingly, from the German invasion in the fall of 1939 until the late summer of 1944, our family remained together, first in the Pabianice ghetto and then in the Lodz ghetto. It was not until we arrived at Auschwitz that we were separated, but even then I remained with my father until about five months before liberation. It was unusual for a family to stay together as long as we did; being with my family sustained me through much of the ordeal of those years. We looked after each other and shielded each other against the hopelessness of our situation.

My father, Yechiel Glass (ca. 1898-1944), was a successful business-man who owned and managed a large textile factory that employed several hundred workers. He worked long hours; even on the Sabbath after the service and dinner, he would go to the factory to make sure that everything was in order. His success made him well known in the community. I remem-ber that people would say, "If you don't know Yechiel Glass, then you are not from Pabianice."

I always looked up to my father. When I visited his factory I felt very proud; I thought that he was incredible, that he could do anything. Now I realize how very difficult it was for him to run his factory with all the restrictions that the extremely anti-Semitic Polish unions imposed on him. Because of union rules, approximately 95 percent of his workers were Polish Gentiles.

My dad was focused on two things, his factory and his family. While he deferred to my mother in most family matters, there was no question that he had the final say in all matters regarding our home. He was very strict with me and my brother and sisters. He had a way of looking at us which com-manded our attention and obedience. All Mom had to say to me was, "I'm going to tell your father," and immediately I stopped whatever foolishness I was up to. Although Dad was strict, he was kind and fair. I was confident that he would care for me and watch over me. He made me feel secure.

My father was a man who was disciplined in his habits. He insisted that the house be spotless and that everything be in the right place. The way he dressed mirrored his insistence on neatness and order. He dressed immaculately; his collars had to be very stiff (they were sent to a special laundry), and everything had to match. Even in the ghetto in Lodz, where hundreds of Jews were dying every day from starvation and disease, he took special care to always be clean shaven and neatly dressed. On the Sabbath he would insist on dressing formally, with matching tiepin and cuff links. Dressing this way gave him pleasure, and, considering the terrible circumstances, I suspect that it reassured him of his human dignity.

My father's clothing also reflected his modern outlook. Shunning the traditional long grey or black coats and hats generally worn by orthodox Jews, he wore modern suits in blues, greens, and browns. Even though I was young, I admired the way my father dressed and was proud of the progressive attitude that his clothes signified.

My dad was too involved in his business to have any hobbies except reading. He loved to read, and he was especially proud of his complete collection of books by Jules Verne. He read them all, and I read most of them, too.

My father spoke fluent German—a skill that would serve us well in the ghettos and camps. However, it was Hebrew, not German, that he insisted I learn. His insistence, I feel certain, stemmed from his commitment to Zionism. Dad always dreamed that someday there would be a Jewish state where Jews would not be kicked around and abused and persecuted and made the laughing stock and blamed for everything that went wrong. At the time his hopes seemed like a fantasy. Unfortunately, he did not live to see his dream come true. He did talk about moving to Palestine but my mom would not consider it.

Father's enthusiasm for Zionism led him to join a Zionist synagogue which was named in honor of Theodore Herzl, the Viennese Jew who founded the Zionist movement in the late 1800s. This synagogue was for men; so only my father, my brother, and I attended it. Although the prohibition against women would suggest otherwise, the men who attended this synagogue were, like my father, modern in dress and in thinking, and the services were performed in a modern way. The congregation and the services at my father's synagogue were worlds apart from those of most Eastern Jews.

Although he attended synagogue every Sabbath as was expected of an observant Jew, my father was not extremely religious. However, he was passionate about a more modern approach to religion, and he was impatient with what he considered to be ultra fanatic approaches to Judaism. When I was about eight or nine there was an election in Pabianice for the position of chief rabbi. The election was important because the chief rabbi more or less controlled the customs involved in keeping a Jewish home and maintaining Jewish culture. In the election, one of the candidates was modern and the other old-fashioned. My dad strongly supported the modern candidate, and he campaigned for his election by printing and distributing leaflets endorsing him. Mom pleaded with him to be quiet because he was in the minority, but Dad continued to campaign. His candidate lost.

My father's religious beliefs caused strained relationships with some of our relatives. No occasion better illustrates this than Dad's distress at having to participate in the arranged wedding of his niece. My uncle was a very orthodox Hasidic Jew who had used a matchmaker to find a husband for his daughter. My eldest sister told me that our cousin had never seen her husband until they were under the canopy at the wedding. Because we were close kin, our family was required to attend an orthodox service on the Sabbath before the wedding. My father was expected to participate in the ceremony, but he swore that he would not. My poor mother, I remember her pleading with him and saying, "Yechiel, it's for the family. This is your niece. We have to go because you will be called upon to read." So we went and Father read. Even though I was a little boy, I remember that he could not wait to leave. Father was not tolerant of ultraorthodox Hasidic Jews.

As much as I loved and admired my father, I spent much more time with my mom who had the day-to-day responsibility of caring for me. Because she was born on Purim, the day that commemorates when the Biblical Queen Esther saved the Jews from the deadly wrath of Haman, she was named Esthera [Esther]. Mom had long, brown hair which she kept in a braid and she was very beautiful. Like my father, she was from Pabianice and her family, like his, had probably migrated from Germany many centuries ago. She was a couple of years younger than Dad; I figure that she was born around 1900. I know that she was old enough to have had vivid memories of World War I because she was continually reminding me that during that war the Germans were the good guys and the Russians were the bad ones. It took awhile for her to accept the fact that the Germans were capable of terrible acts.

My mom was a gentle and kind lady and a wonderful mother. She took good care of me even though I was a mischievous boy who must have tried her patience. Although Father did occasionally administer well-deserved spankings, only once did my mom lay a hand on me. What provoked her was that I had lied about belonging to a Zionist youth group, membership in which was forbidden. Had I been discovered, I would have been expelled from school. The minute she hit me, I could tell that Mom regretted what she had done. She never told my dad that I had lied.

When I would come home after I had been beaten up, my mom would treat me ever so gently and tenderly. She would take cold towels and lay them on the places where I had been hit, and she would soothe my hurt feelings by explaining that only a few individuals act this way, and that most people are good. Not only was she kind to her family but she also had a heart full of charity for those who were less fortunate. As was the custom in Poland on Thursdays and Fridays, many beggars, predominantly Jews but also some Gentiles, came to our door. They were never disappointed. In fact, there were so many beggars that one of my chores was to help Mom distribute money and goods to them.

Taking care of the poor was a religious imperative for my mother, an obligation she felt deeply. She also kept a strictly kosher home. She carefully prepared the meals and the house before Friday evening so that no work would take place on the Sabbath. Mom attended a large synagogue that admitted males and females but required the women to sit in a separate area. She did not go every Sabbath; in fact, she only attended on the high holy days. But even then, my father never attended services with her. I don't know why— that is just the way it was. Although my mom did not regularly attend the synagogue, she was more religious than my dad. I remember in the ghetto that, when I had my bar mitzvah and Mom insisted that I wrap my arms and say certain prayers, my father commented, "What do you want from this child? There is a war going on." I did it for the ceremony but she never asked me to do it again.

My parents had well-defined roles in the family. Dad was the lord of the house, the breadwinner, and the person who sat at the head of the table. But my mom ran the household, and, at least in my presence, my father never interfered or raised his voice or said anything unkind to her. My mom worshiped him and he obviously adored her—it was a good marriage. Neither of my parents survived.

Outside of our many family gatherings, my parents enjoyed socializing with their friends. They belonged to a group of about six couples who would gather on Saturday night to eat, talk, play cards, and listen to music. They had a good time.

While my parents enjoyed a close relationship with each other, their relationship with my sisters, brother, and me was distant. I think this distance reflected the custom in Europe at the time. As a result, the person in my family to whom I was closest was not my mother or father but my sister

Rozka [Rachael]. I simply adored her! She was gorgeous, absolutely gorgeous, with the brown hair and brown eyes that were a Glass family trait. Because she was so beautiful and dynamic, folks would say, "When Rozka Glass walks the streets, she rips the stones out."

I talked to Rozka about everything. She tried to teach me to be forgiving and kind and to find the good in everyone. When Yom Kippur, the Day of Atonement, neared, Rozka would tell me, "Morris, if you have argued with anyone or feel that you have done something that may have offended somebody, you must walk over to them and shake hands and ask for their forgiveness." When I had unpleasant experiences because of being Jewish, I felt much more comfortable talking to her about them than to my mom or dad. When I would tell Rozka about some incident, she would say, "Morris, It's going to be better when you grow up." It meant a lot to me that I could confide in her.

We also had fun together. Rozka knew that I loved ice cream, so as a special treat she would take me to an ice cream store in Lodz. What a fantasy of colors and flavors! I remember always choosing a popsicle with vanilla ice cream dipped in chocolate. These outings with Rozka are amongst my happiest memories!

For many, many years after the war, I refused to believe that Rozka did not survive. She was young, beautiful and healthy and I kept thinking that someday I would see her again, that she would miraculously appear. I imagined all kinds of scenarios to explain her absence. Maybe she had married a Gentile and was ashamed to tell the family. Perhaps she had escaped to Russia and couldn't return. Perhaps she was simply unable to find me. For years I grasped at any fantasy that would keep me from facing the truth—Rozka was dead.

While I loved my other sister and my brother, I was never as close to them as I was to Rozka. My sister Bluma [Florence] was nearest to me in age, and, like me, she loved school and was a very good student. When the war began, she was attending high school in Lodz. She also did not survive. The one member of my immediate family who did survive was my brother Nachman [Nathan]. We were separated at Auschwitz but after the war I found him in Germany. In 1949 he immigrated to the United States with me.

Among the possessions that I most treasure is a picture of my parents and my older sister that was taken around 1936. It is the only picture that I have of my parents. Most survivors have no photographs so I consider myself extremely fortunate. This photograph, along with one of Rozka and one of Bluma, was saved by a friend who fled to Russia and who gave them to me after the war. It is hard to express just how very precious these two photographs are to me. [See photographs at the end of the chapter.]

The only grandparent I knew was my mother's mother, Grandmother Kupperwasser, and unfortunately what I remember most clearly about her is her death and funeral. She died on August 30, 1939, two days before the German invasion, and was buried on August 31, the day before the war began. I remember her funeral well because as Mother, Bluma, and I walked to the cemetery, Polish soldiers were rapidly marching past us in the opposite direction headed toward the German border. I also remember that my father, Rozka, and Nachman could not attend because they were busily assembling everything that the government had instructed us to prepare for the anticipated attack. Thanks to their efforts when the war began, I had a backpack filled with everything that the Polish government deemed necessary for survival. I wish that survival had been that simple.

Grandmother Kupperwasser left behind a large family. At the beginning of the war, my mom had five siblings, all of whom lived in Pabianice or Lodz; combined they had sixteen children. We spent holidays and celebrated special occasions with our Kupperwasser uncles, aunts, and cousins—I felt very close to them. Counting our family, the Kupperwasser family in Poland before the war, numbered thirty-two persons. The only survivor besides my brother and me was a cousin who fled to Russia at the beginning of the war. From Russia she somehow went to China and finally to Australia. Otherwise, no one else survived. No one.

The only member of the Kupperwasser family who left the area before the war was Mom's youngest brother Mordechai who immigrated to Palestine when he was eighteen. Sadly, not long after he arrived, Mordechai contracted malaria while helping to dry out swampland in the Golan Heights and died. Because he immigrated to Palestine during the early years, Mordechai was considered one if the "pioneers" of Israel and is buried in the Tumpeldor Cemetery in Tel Aviv, a special cemetery where many of the early settlers are buried. It was because of her brother's early death that Mom refused to listen when Father tried to persuade her to leave Poland and go to Palestine.

My father's immediate family consisted of a sister and three brothers; Father was the youngest child. The only one of his siblings who was living in Poland when the war began was his sister, Bleema, who also lived in Pabianice. Bleema had four children and three grandchildren—none survived. My father's three brothers had all left Poland long before the war.

His eldest brother, Harry, immigrated to the United States around 1914; it was he who brought my brother and me to the States in 1949. Another brother, Shcomo, had immigrated to Sweden, where he died before the war began. The third brother, Izsak, had moved to Paris. During the war he and his wife, Chana, were deported to Auschwitz where he was killed. Chana survived as did their two children, who were sheltered by French Gentiles. After the war, Chana and the children moved to Montreal. I remained close to my aunt until her death two months shy of her one-hundredth birthday.

In addition to the Glass relatives mentioned above, my father had an uncle, Bernard, who moved to Germany in the 1920s. At that time Germany had a democratic government and a tolerant society, and Uncle Bernard settled down, established a medical practice, and raised his family there. Bernard thought highly of Germany; in fact, he considered himself to be German. But his life there began to change in 1933 when Hitler gained power and the Nazis began to exclude the Jews from German life and to persecute them. Finally in 1938, the Nazis expelled all Polish-born Jews and forced them to return to Poland; among those exiled were Bernard and his son Max.[2] My father met them at the border and brought them to live with us. Neither survived the Holocaust. Despite his suffering at the hands of the Nazis, Uncle Bernard proudly admitted to being a German.

I cannot account for all of my third cousins, but the story of one, Natek Glass, is especially interesting. Before the war, Natek was well known in the textile industry in Pabianice; he was well educated and handsome, and he looked Aryan. When the war began, Natek decided to meld into the Gentile population. He adopted a Polish name, obtained forged papers and moved with his wife and child to a town where no one knew him. There, he and his family lived as Christians, attending church and even placing a crucifix over the baby's crib. After the war when Natek returned to Pabianice and attempted to resume his old life, an anti-Semitic group discovered his past and twice tried to kill him. Finally, he and his family escaped from Poland and immigrated to Australia. Even though he was far from Poland, Natek remained fearful. Either because of his fears or for other reasons, he subsequently committed suicide.

Outside of our family, the one person who was close to me and my family when I was a child was our maid, Steffa. Steffa—I'm ashamed that I cannot remember her family name—worked for my family for about seventeen years. She was attractive and neat, and she always wore a blanket around her shoulders to keep warm. She was unfailingly kind to me; she dressed me for school and took me to play in the parks. I especially remem-

ber one time when I was five or six when she took me to a special mass at her church. It was the first time that I was ever in a Christian church, and I was scared to death. I had never seen anything like it—special uniforms, holy water—it was incredible. She may have taken me other times, but this is the only service that I remember.

Steffa lived at our house and slept in the kitchen. She mainly cooked and cleaned; another woman washed our clothes and linens. Steffa would go home on Saturday after everything was prepared for the Sabbath and return on Sunday evening. Following the German conquest, even though she was no longer allowed to work for us, she remained loyal to my family and tried to help us. When we were placed in the ghetto, she continued to visit and to bring us food. I remember that she would cry when she left. We of course paid her, but, nevertheless, bringing us food was not without danger. She was indeed around "Righteous Gentiles." After we left the Pabianice ghetto, I never saw her again. For that matter, neither did I ever again see any of my relatives from Pabianice.

1. The boundary between Germany and Poland has been changed many times. In 1939 the eastern border of Germany extended much farther into western Poland than at present. During much of the 19th century through the end of World War I, there was no Poland. What had formerly been Poland was divided between Russia, Austria-Hungary, and Prussia—Prussia was later absorbed into the new state of Germany. Pabianice and the western areas of Poland were included in the land allotted to Prussia/Germany.

2. "Uncle Bernard's wife died before the war. He had a daughter who immigrated to Palestine before the war and a son who immigrated to the United States before the war." Morris Glass

Morris's parents and eldest sister, Rozka, before the war.

Morris's eldest sister Rozka before the war.

Morris's sister Bluma wearing a hat bearing the insignia of her school.

Chapter 4

My Childhood

I was a child of the Diaspora, a Jew living in Christian Poland. This fact shaped my early years. On the one hand, I had a very happy childhood within the confines of a loving and prosperous family; on the other, I experienced heartache and fear stemming from the deep well of anti-Semitism that permeated Polish life. Morris Glass

I was born on April 3, 1928. I never liked my birthday—too close to Passover. There was too much attention to preparing matzo and not enough attention to me—or at least that is how I felt as a child. The things I most remember from my childhood are food, school, friends, games, books, movies, vacations, holidays, and the constant reminders that I was a Jew, different and unwanted.

I was a skinny kid who just didn't like to eat, or at least who didn't like to eat healthy foods. I loved sweets—cookies, waffles, ice cream, and, above all, chocolate. My mom tried very hard to give me nutritious foods. Each day she would prepare rolls for me to take to school, and each day I would give them away and then stop at a store where our family had an account and buy something sweet to eat. Mom plied me with cod-liver oil and vitamins and took me to health spas and special doctors; she was really concerned about me. But I remained a picky eater and a skinny kid. It is strange but when we were starving in the ghettos and the camps—it is impossible to describe just how hungry we were—I was never obsessed, as most people were, by food. Maybe the fact that I had never much cared about eating helped me to survive—I don't know.

Mom made sure that I dressed immaculately and that I always had a clean handkerchief. She combed my hair with a small-tooth comb several times a week to make sure that I was free of lice. Lice were everywhere. Because they were such a nuisance, officials checked our hair twice a week and sent home any students on whom they found lice. I felt embarrassed and sorry for those students, and, as I really, really did not want to be among them, I gladly endured the constant combings. Mom also made sure that we all had a bath on Thursday evenings. Since we had to heat the water on a stove, taking a bath was a complicated process. As the youngest child, I had the advantage of bathing first and thus enjoyed a tub of hot, clean water. During the Holocaust, when I went for years and years without a hot bath, I would dream about sitting in that tub of hot, soapy water.

I loved school! I couldn't wait to get up in the morning to go. Learning was easy for me and I was a very good student. I went to a public elementary school where the students were almost exclusively Jewish, as were most, but not all, of our teachers. Our principal was a kind Gentile whom I liked very much. There was another elementary school that was also primarily Jewish. Each school had a number; our school was number eight and the other Jewish school was thirteen. Since we wore hats with our school number on them, Jews were easily identified. Pabianice was small, so there was no Jewish high school. Since it took a lot of courage for a Jew to attend a Gentile school, most Jews, including my brother and sisters, rode the trolley to Lodz to attend the Jewish high school there.

Although I really liked school, there were a lot of other things I enjoyed too. I guess my favorite pastime was playing soccer; I would hurry through my homework so that I could go out and play. Since there were no special soccer fields, we played in empty lots and used our clothes and book bags to mark the borders and the goals. In short, we played anywhere and anytime we could.

I also loved going to the movies. From Tuesday through Thursday, the theaters showed special films for children, mainly cowboy, Tarzan, and Zorro films. I really looked forward to the movies and went almost every week. My favorite cowboys were Ken Maynard, Buck Jones, Tom Tyler and Tom Mix. When I came to America and saw Ken Maynard—well, I just can't tell you how excited I was to see my childhood hero. It was a dream come true! Johnny Weissmuller was Tarzan and a favorite, and I also loved Buster Keaton and Charlie Chaplin. I especially remember Errol Flynn in The Charge of the Light Brigade and Cary Grant in Gunga Din. In both movies, Brits were the heroes, and this fit our understanding of the British as the kings of the world. As for the Americans— well, we thought they were great, and we loved them because of the cowboys and Tarzan and all of the Hollywood movies. But it was the British whom we regarded as supermen who could do anything. I remember how secure it made us feel when Britain declared war on Germany after the Germans invaded Poland in 1939.

While we admired the British, it was the cowboys and Indians and the settlers in the American West that more than anything else captured our imagination. My friends and I read everything we could find about them. The weekly magazines for young people had many stories about the American West, and we would eagerly look forward to reading and discussing each new edition. We knew about the Sioux and the Comanche and some of the smaller tribes, but I realize now that we really did not have a very good understanding about the American Indians. Then, however, that did not matter. We loved to concoct scenarios about the American West and imitate the settlers, the cowboys, and the Indians. I had a special talent for imagining plots, figuring out ambushes, and generally causing chaos in the Wild West. We made hats from paper and guns from wood. It was great fun. One of my friends who had lived in Germany had a real toy gun and also lead soldiers and Indians. Everybody begged him to let them play with these toys, toys we never dreamed existed before he arrived with them.

In addition to our fantasy games, we played regular games like bingo, Monopoly, and pick-up sticks and card games like Black Peter and Rat King. We would play makeshift ping-pong on the dining room table with a broom for the net and paddles that we made from plywood. It was crude but it worked. One of my favorite games was one where each person was given a letter after which he had to name a city, country, river, flower, and vegetable that began with the same letter. It was fun and educational, and since it did not require a board or equipment, we played it often after we were in the ghettoes.

My favorite time of the year was summer. Summers were spent in villas that our family rented in the countryside about an hour's ride from Pabianice. This was heaven—there was lots of time for soccer, swimming, biking, games, and making new friends. Most of my friends were Jewish, but some were Gentiles. In the countryside we played with the Gentile boys and girls; we went to their homes, and they went to ours. This would never have happened in the city. I had no Gentile friends in Pabianice other than a few I occasionally played soccer with. Some summers, we would also go *to the mountains. Mom was always fretting because I was so skinny, and she thought that the mountain water was good for my health.*

And then there were the Sabbath dinners and the holidays—Passover, Hanukkah, and Purim; these were the occasion for great times. One of the happiest moments of the week was the evening of the Sabbath. The evening began with the traditional Sabbath dinner featuring candles, prayers, wine, and delicious food. Dessert was an array of sweets—that was the best part! My dad always had tea. His tea was served boiling hot in a thin glass with a silver spoon to absorb the heat; I always wondered how he could drink something so hot. After dinner we would go into the living room and dance. My brother and I would dance with my mom and my dad would dance with my sisters. Then the children would dance with each other. Sometimes we would also play games. These were happy times!

My favorite holiday was Hanukkah in December. Everyone—parents, siblings, aunts, and uncles—all gave me money, and we spun the dreidel, played games, and lit the Menorah candles. Passover, in the spring, was also a happy holiday. It meant new clothes—everyone had to have new clothes—visiting with my aunts, uncles, and cousins, and eating lots of good food. Passover was fun for me, but it must have been a lot of work for my mom. She had to clean and polish everything in the house and take out of storage the special pots and pans that she used only for the Passover meals. She also had to prepare the matzo [unleavened bread]. At first, the matzo tasted good, but after several days the novelty wore off and it didn't taste so great.

Because my mom was born on Purim, the holiday commemorating when Queen Esther saved the ancient Jews from annihilation, she was named Esther. Consequently, Purim became an excuse for my family to host a big celebration. All of our relatives and my parents' friends would come to our apartment wearing costumes and masks, and we would eat potato pancakes and read the story of Esther, the Jewish heroine. The other holidays, Rosh Hashanah, the Jewish New Year, and Yom Kippur, the Day of Atonement, were serious and somber Holy Days. They were not festive occasions for the enjoyment of children.

The happy times, and there were many, occurred within the context of my family and the Jewish community. My experiences in the larger Gentile world were quite different—it is difficult to describe the heartaches that I experienced as a child. Anti-Semitism was in the air, and I encountered it in many forms. Verbal taunts like "Dirty Jew," "Christ Killer," and "Go back to Palestine" were the most common expressions of anti-Semitism. But violence was also routine, and little children were not exempt from it.

One of my favorite pastimes, going to the movies, was often spoiled by anti-Semitic acts—names, threats and beatings were common. Nevertheless, my friends and I looked forward to going to the movies every week even though our excitement was tempered by fear. Often as we approached the theater, we would see groups of older Gentile boys wait-ing to bait us. We would try to hide our identity by taking off our hats with our school number emblazoned on them, and we would call each other by Gentile names like Valdi or Steffan. Despite our efforts, the Polish boys would still recognize us, and they would force us to pay them a bribe to en-ter the theater. But the worst treatment would come after the film was over. Because of this we learned to sense when a movie was ending, and then to move quietly toward the exit in hopes of escaping before the Gentile boys left. Once outside, we would run away as fast as we could. Sometimes this strategy worked but often it didn't. I could run fast, but others, like my best friend Abraham who was quite heavy and very slow, were not so fortunate.

One time after a movie, when I was about nine or ten, some Gentile boys caught Abraham and beat him badly. He had blood all over him. We hurriedly wiped away the blood and ran from the side street where the theater was located to the main street. Here we saw a policeman. Since the Polish boys were still following us, we went to the policeman and told him what had happened. "Who did this to you?" he asked, and we pointed to the group of boys. The officer then asked them, "Why did you beat him up?" They said, "Well, he is a Jew boy." "Oh, well, that's okay," shrugged the officer. This was a response we heard or intuited many times; it was just the way it was growing up a Jew in Poland.

Much like going to the movies, playing soccer also had its dangers. Whenever we played soccer, we would have one eye on the ball and with the other watch for Polish boys. When even two or three approached us, we would grab everything and run for our lives. We wanted to stand up to them, but we realized that it was hopeless; we knew that no one would protect us or come to our rescue. Usually, I ran fast enough to get away, but occasionally I was caught and beaten. When this happened, as I have said before, my mom would calmly take cold towels and lay them on the hurt places to lessen the pain. In her kind way she would try to comfort me. She would tell me that only a few individuals were so cruel, but I wasn't so sure that she was right. I do know that even at a very young age, I felt fear. It was a feeling that was reinforced many, many times.

One of those times that I particularly remember occurred during a soccer match between some older Gentile and Jewish boys. Both teams had good players, and my friends and I and many others went out to watch the game, which was played in an abandoned field without real goalposts and nets. Shortly after the game began, we thought one of the Jewish boys had scored a goal, and we all cheered and yelled, "Goal! Goal!" This angered the Gentiles. They started heaving stones at us and many of us were injured. I was hit in the leg but one of our players was hit in the eye, and blood gushed everywhere. All of us, even the older boys, just picked up our things and ran. The game was over just because we had yelled, "Goal."

Running when provoked was a response which my friends and I learned from experience; it was also drummed into us by every adult. As a child it seemed to me that a dozen times a week someone—either my father, or an uncle, or my older brother or sisters— told me, "Do not fight back." My dad explained that not responding was a way of protecting myself against greater violence. He said that if I fought back, I might be killed. We wanted to fight. We weren't cowards. But we were told not to, and, furthermore, we knew that no one would come to our rescue. So we ran away— at the first sign of trouble, we ran as fast as we could. That's the way I remember it, and it is something that has stayed with me the rest of my life.

There were many more anti-Semitic episodes in my early life, but two in particular illuminate the pain and humiliation that I experienced. When I was nine, I wanted a real soccer ball, one made of leather. A ball like that cost a lot of money, so I saved and saved until finally I could buy the ball of my dreams. I was so happy and so proud of my beautiful, new soccer ball; unfortunately my happiness was short lived. One afternoon, not long after I had bought the ball, Abraham and I were tossing it back and forth as we walked home from school. Suddenly, one of us dropped it, and my precious ball rolled into the street. Before I could retrieve it, a wagon with two horses loaded with piece goods drove by and I saw the driver deliberately take his whip and move the ball so that the wagon would run over it. My beautiful ball was crushed beneath the wagon's wheels! The driver laughed and laughed; he thought it was very funny. He knew that I was Jewish. I was brokenhearted; I cried and cried and cried. It was a small act, but it broke my young heart.

While the destruction of my soccer ball hurt me, another incident which I cannot forget is one that humiliated all of the Jewish children of Pabianice. This incident was connected with a celebration of the 1936 Olympics, and it illustrates how widespread and deeply embedded anti-Semitism was. After the Olympics were over, some of the outstanding Polish athletes toured the country. Several were scheduled to come to Pabianice, and a huge festival was organized to honor them. All of the elementary students were asked to march and perform gymnastics during the celebration. We were all required to wear the same outfit—black shorts, white shirts, and white hats.

I was so excited to be part of such a big event, and, since our school was Jewish, we were very anxious to do ourselves proud. We practiced and practiced so as not to make even the smallest mistake; we wanted to be perfect. We took our performance very seriously because we knew that the Jewish community as a whole would be judged by what we did. During the rehearsals with the other schools, the Gentile students jeered, called us names, and spit on us when we marched onto the field. Practices were excruciating, but I was certain that on the day of the ceremony it would be different. Yet even on that day, a day when we were so proud to be Polish and when we were all dressed alike, the taunts and spitting persisted. Thankfully, we performed perfectly but our pride was mingled with humiliation. Despite being treated in this manner, we loved our country and were proud to be citizens of Poland.

Even though we loved our country, the daily insults and the declarations that we were not wanted made me and many other Jews receptive to Zionism and its call for the creation of a Jewish state in Palestine. The dream of a day when we would have a homeland of our own, where Jews would not be ostracized and made to feel as though they had horns and two left hands, was appealing, indeed. This was especially true for eastern European Jews who had been targeted for wholesale violence in the late 19th century. Since my father was an avid Zionist and my uncle had immigrated to Palestine, it is not surprising that I would have been interested in this movement when I was very young. Despite the fact that children were forbidden to belong to a Zionist organization, I joined a group. The meetings were all very innocent; we sang, danced, talked about Jewish heroes and about Herzl, and dreamed. But, we were in no way activists—I was only about ten. Nevertheless, I kept my membership a secret from my parents. As I related earlier, my mom somehow found out, and I immediately quit my group.

The anti-Semitic episodes from my childhood, painful though they were, were just the prelude to the horror that was to follow. The Nazi conquest of western Poland in 1939 and of eastern Poland in the summer of 1941 was accompanied by terror and murder on a scale unprecedented in history. Nothing in the experience of the European Jews prepared us *for the destruction that was to come; we could not have forecast or even imagined the destruction that would be visited upon us. Ironically, one of the results of the Holocaust would be the realization of the Zionist dream of an independent Jewish state. In 1948, three years after the defeat of Nazi Germany, the state of Israel was created.*

Chapter 5

The War Begins

Early in the morning of Friday, September 1, 1939, the German army invaded Poland. Thus began a war that changed my life and that of millions of other people, Jew and Gentile, Pole and non-Pole, forever. It brought an end to my childhood and flung me into a nightmare that lasted until I was liberated by the American army some five and a half years later. Morris Glass

When World War II ended in May, 1945 some fifty million people were dead, many millions had been wounded and displaced, and much of Europe was reduced to rubble. Among the dead were six million Jews who had been murdered by the Nazis and their accomplices. Over three million of these were Polish Jews—90 percent of the prewar Jewish population. Poland lost more Jews and a larger percentage of Jews than any other country.[1] Located at the geographical heart of the murders, Poland was the site of the six killing centers, Auschwitz-Birkenau, Treblinka, Chelmno, Sobibor, Belzec, and Majdanek, where Jews from Poland and all over Europe were gassed. It was not only Jews who were murdered by the Nazis; among their other victims were gypsies, homosexuals, Jehovah's Witnesses, Polish Gentiles, Slavs, and Soviet POWs.

Both the war and the murder were predictable, inevitable outcomes of Nazi ideology. Hitler had always asserted the need for Germany to expand her territory at the expense of other people; this expansion mandated war. And Nazism's radical doctrine envisioning the creation of a Master Race of Aryans mandated the elimination of the Jews and other inferior peoples. Murder was adopted only after other strategies had failed. Genocide was indeed the Final Solution to the Jewish problem.

The signs of the approaching war were easy to see, even for someone as young as I, but the signs of the murder that would accompany it were less obvious. Genocide on such a scale was unfathomable; it was simply beyond human comprehension. And so for some time, we lived with the knowledge that war was inevitable, and that it would probably not be pleasant for the Jews. Nevertheless, knowing that we had survived bad times in the past, we thought that we would survive this bad period also. A few, like my uncle Mordechai, left for Palestine or other places. But most— those without the means or too entangled with family— stayed.

We knew what was happening to the Jews in Germany; the Nazis did not try to hide their actions. In Poland we read about the anti-Semitic de- crees and incidents. At the movies we watched the Nazi rallies with all the flags and lights, and we saw the endless parades and heard Hitler speak- ing on the radio. Furthermore, our family, like many others in Poland, had relatives in Germany who reported developments there. My parents talked about the situation in Germany, and, as far as I know, they never tried to hide what was happening from my siblings and me. At first they dismissed Hitler's rantings as just posturing and meaningless rhetoric, a way to gain and hold power. They tended to dismiss events in Germany as just another episode in a long history of discrimination and persecution that, like the other episodes, would pass over. Furthermore, anti-Semitism was growing in Poland, so comparatively, the situation in Germany did not seem that frightening. I remember my mom saying, "Look, it can't get any worse than it is now. How much worse can it get?"

But in the second half of 1938, events in Germany took an ominous turn. First, all of the Jews who had been born in Poland were expelled in the fall of 1938, among them Uncle Bernard and cousin Max. From them we heard first-hand accounts of the increasing isolation, ostracism, and abuse of the German Jews. Cousin Max talked about how difficult it had been to attend school and about how some of his best friends, many of them childhood friends from his neighborhood, had turned against him. He kept repeating this because he could not believe that it had happened. His stories were about experiences that I could relate to, and they deepened my sensitivity to the situation of the Jews in Germany.

Then, one night in November shortly after Uncle Bernard and Max had been expelled, the Nazis went on a rampage of violence throughout Germany. They broke windows and looted Jewish stores, burned synagogues, entered Jewish homes and smashed the furniture, and generally terrorized the German Jews. This night of terror, known as Kristallnacht, was a sobering event for both the Jews and the Gentiles in Germany and elsewhere. It certainly affected my father's outlook; he became more grave. I recall him saying, "We are facing very sad times. Things are going to get worse. The future doesn't look bright." He began to talk about immigrating to Palestine, but Mom did not want to go because her brother had died there. As my father became more and more insistent, she kept repeating, "I don't want to hear about it. I don't want to hear about it."

I am sure Father was aware of how very difficult it would be to immigrate. First, it was practically impossible to find a country that would allow Jews to enter. Second, it would be painful to leave a tight-knit family and venture into a new life. So we stayed. But as Hitler began to rave more and more about expansion eastward and to back up his words with actions, I could tell that my parents had become more and more worried.

Hitler's aggressions escalated rapidly. First, in March 1938, Germany incorporated Austria into the Third Reich. Almost immediately afterward, Hitler began demanding the German-speaking, western region of Czechoslovakia, known as the Sudetenland. Regrettably, Britain and France agreed to Hitler's demands, and the area was absorbed into the Third Reich. I remember well the headlines in the paper during the Munich Crisis—"ABCD in Munich," Adolf, Benito (Mussolini), Chamberlin (Prime Minister of Britain), Daladier (Premier of France). Early in 1939, Hitler predictably seized the rest of Czechoslovakia and began to threaten Poland.

My father kept saying, "God help us." Still, many Poles, including my mom, were sure that our defensive treaty with Britain would protect us against invasion. They were sure that Hitler would not dare go to war against the mighty British. As German threats became louder and more insistent, Poland made it clear that she would not give up without a fight. "We will not give up, even a button," was Poland's answer to Germany. Although it might seem somewhat contradictory, the Poles were at the same time very anti-Semitic and very anti-German.

By the summer of 1939, Nazi rhetoric had increased to such a level that war seemed inevitable. But still we hoped. When the Non-Aggression Treaty between Germany and the Soviet Union was announced on August 23, we knew that Germany would shortly attack Poland. On hearing about the treaty, Father expressed the general consensus, "Now there will be war."

Immediately, we hurried to complete the preparations that the Polish government had been urging us to make. Father bought a gas mask for each of us, and we sealed one of the bedrooms so that it would be gas proof. We provisioned our home with water and dry bread, and we prepared the backpacks containing the items recommended for survival. I helped to dig a hole in our backyard with a camouflaged top for use during air raids, and Father had a six-foot ditch dug around his factory. While I was aware of just how grave the situation was, my friends and I could not resist playing war in the newly dug ditch—I was only eleven.

As expected, the invasion came shortly after the Non-Aggression Treaty was announced. The day it occurred is one of many days that is frozen in my memory. Our home, which was already somber because of my grandmother's death, became deadly quiet on the morning of September 1, when the radio announced that the Germans had crossed the Polish border. All day long, my parents stayed glued to the radio. Father encouraged us to read and do other things, but my brother, sisters, and I stayed close to the radio as well. Mother, ever the optimist, buoyed us by repeating that all was not lost; that the British would intervene and save Poland. Father, ever the realist, was mostly concerned that we stay close together and always wear our backpacks.

For the first several days after the invasion, everything seemed eerily quiet, and nothing seemed changed. We continued to stay close to home and to listen to the radio. We rejoiced on learning that Britain and France had declared war against Germany—maybe Poland would be saved after all. But that was wishful thinking. The truth came in the form of radio reports describing the steady German advance.

On the fifth or sixth day after the invasion, a bomb fell near our apartment. The war suddenly became real and I was scared, really scared. The radio began announcing how close the army was to our town, and it also announced the Polish government's decision to wait until the Germans reached Warsaw to mount an all-out defense. And so the Wehrmacht moved steadily eastward, virtually unopposed, through western Poland, including Pabianice and neighboring Lodz. When it reached the outskirts of Warsaw, the Polish army fought bravely for almost six weeks before finally surrendering in October.

In the meantime, in accordance with her agreement with Germany, the Soviet Union invaded Poland from the east, and soon Poland was divided between the two countries. My town was in that part of Poland that fell under German control. Later in the summer of 1941, following Germany's surprise attack on the Soviet Union, the Germans would occupy the rest of Poland. It was at this point that the Nazis began the total destruction of Europe's Jews. But that was two years in the future. Meanwhile, my family and I were now under the control of the Nazis experiencing a preview of what was to come.

My first direct contact with the Germans occurred about the second week of September 1939, when the Wehrmacht hurriedly marched through Pabianice on its way to Warsaw. What an impressive and terrifying sight the German army was! From a side street, my friends and I watched in awe as hour after hour a seemingly endless and incredibly powerful force of motorcycles, trucks, and tanks moved quickly through our town. Pabianice seemed to shake at the might of this fast-moving army. Never had I seen such fearsome power; never had I seen such a frightening spectacle. It seemed that the Germans were truly a race of giants. The army moved on, and in its wake German officials came and took control of Pabianice. That night Father said to us, "Do not leave the house." We did not need his warning. Rumors that the Germans had already shot some Hasidic Jews were warning enough.

During the first days of the Nazi occupation, the town was very quiet. We stayed inside and listened to the radio and tried to occupy ourselves. Then on about the third day, the Nazis set fire to the main synagogue and the sacred scriptures and prayer robes. The synagogue was only about a block from our house on the opposite side of Warsaw Street, and I could easily watch as it burned. Even though I had seen pictures and read about the destruction of the synagogues in Germany, it was a shock to see this happening in my town. For the first time since the war began, I felt personally threatened because I was Jewish. The smiles and amusement evidenced by many of the Gentiles who gathered to watch the spectacle was a chilling revelation that added to my terror. Later, the Germans used the shell of the synagogue as a stable. Nothing remains of it today except some walls and a plaque commemorating the former synagogue.

Further developments intensified my fears. Shortly after the burning of the synagogue, radios and telephones were taken away from both Jews and Gentiles. We now had to rely on word of mouth for news. In addition, the Jews were forced to surrender all books. I helped my father throw his precious library out of a window of our apartment and watched with him as the Nazis burned his books in the street below. I will never forget the tears *that welled in his eyes as he watched his precious books go up in flames.*

Father suffered further heartbreak a few weeks later when one of his workers came to him with a letter stating that the Germans had turned over our factory to him. The worker ordered father to leave immediately and not to return. This man was a German who, like many others, had moved to Poland after World War I because of the hard economic times in Germany. There were many people like him living in western Poland, and the conquering Nazis made good use of them. Before this happened, the Germans had forced some Hasidic Jews to fill in the defensive trench around Father's factory with their bare hands.

The Jews of Pabianice were not ordered to live in a ghetto until the spring of 1940, but our living conditions nevertheless continued to deteriorate. We were denied the right to go to school, stores, the movies, libraries, and parks. We had to wear armbands and, later, Stars of David on the outside of our clothing. When we passed a German, we had to take off our hats and bow. If we didn't, we might be hit or beaten. I was hit on the head only once, but beatings occurred frequently and were sometimes brutal, sadistic, and deadly. The Germans seemed to take special pleasure in mocking and ridiculing old men with beards. Jews were also forced to perform random jobs for the Germans like cleaning homes and stables and filling in ditches. Some were taken outside the town to do hard labor.

We, and also the Polish Gentiles, were forbidden to speak Polish to the Germans; the penalty was death. Somewhat to my amazement, while the Germans forbade Polish, they allowed us to speak Yiddish, maybe because it was derived from German. Since most Jews spoke Yiddish, we were able to manage; I think the language restriction was more difficult for the Polish Gentiles. But it was best to speak German, and so I began trying to learn it. Although I never studied German in any formal way, I was able to pick it up from my father and other random people. My best teacher was my German supervisor in the factory where I worked in Lodz, but that was later. Learning German was a plus for me, especially during the last year of the war when I was imprisoned in southern Germany.

Considering the deteriorating situation in our town, in December 1939, Father decided to send Mother, Bluma, and me to Belchatow, a small town southeast of Pabianice in an area known as the Protectorate. The Protectorate was an area of Poland that had been conquered by Germany but, unlike the area around my hometown, had not been incorporated into the German state. Father thought that we would be freer and safer there. Indeed, the German presence in Belchatow was not as obvious, and I was less afraid. However, life was boring. It was winter and cold, and I missed my friends and the rest of my family. So, I was happy when Father summoned us back to Pabianice in March 1940. He wanted us to come back because it was rumored that a ghetto was to be formed and he feared that we might not be able to return once it was completed. So we returned, and shortly thereafter, as Father had predicted, the ghetto became a reality.

I was to live in a ghetto for four and a half years from the early spring of 1940 to the late summer of 1944. I was among the first Jews to be forced into a ghetto and I was among the last Jews to be deported from one.

1. Although statistics on the number of Jews killed during the Holocaust vary, there is substantial agreement as to the numbers. The table below is from Lucy S. Dawidowicz, *The War Against the Jews*, 1933-1945, New York: Bantam Books, 1986, Appendix B, "The Final Solution in Figures," p. 403.

Estimated Number of Jews Killed in the Final Solution

Country	Estimated Pre-Final Solution Population	Estimated Jewish Population Annihilated	Percent
Poland	3,300,000	3,000,000	90
Baltic Countries	253,000	228,000	90
Germany/Austria	240,000	210,000	90
Protectorate	90,000	80,000	89
Slovakia	90,000	75,000	83
Greece	70,000	54,000	77
The Netherlands	140,000	105,000	75
Hungary	650,000	450,000	70
SSR White Russia	375,000	245,000	65
SSR Ukraine	1,500,000	900,000	60
Belgium	65,000	40,000	60
Yugoslavia	43,000	26,000	60
Rumania	600,000	300,000	50
Norway	1,800	900	50
France	350,000	90,000	26
Bulgaria	64,000	14,000	22
Italy	40,000	8,000	20
Luxembourg	5,000	1,000	20
Russia (RSFSR)	975,000	107,000	11
Denmark	8,000	---	---
Finland	2,000	---	---

Chapter 6

The Pabianice Ghetto

For four and a half years, from 1940 to 1944, I lived in Jewish ghettos, first in my hometown, Pabianice, and then in neighboring Lodz. I was almost twelve when my confinement began, and I was sixteen and a half when it ended. In the intervening years I came to know well the grim reality of ghetto life—it was a life of hunger, disease, filth, fear, and death. Because the conditions were so deplorable, many people died from starvation, malnutrition, and disease while confined in the ghettos.[1] Along with the other ghetto dwellers, my family suffered greatly. But somehow we survived. Wretched as our situation was, as long as we were together and able to sustain and comfort one another, life had meaning. Morris Glass

Ghettos, or as they have also been known, "the Jewish Quarter," were not new to the Holocaust. Restriction to certain areas had been a feature of Jewish life for many centuries, at least since the 1500s, when the ghetto made famous by Shakespeare in *The Merchant of Venice* came into existence. Although ghettos were subject to the laws of the area in which they were located, the Jews generally ruled themselves within them. The Nazis used this tradition of self-government to their advantage during the Holocaust.

As Jews, especially those in western Europe, increasingly assimilated into the Gentile population in the nineteenth century, ghettos began to disappear in the West. But when the venomously anti-Semitic Nazis came to power, they resurrected the ghetto and made it an integral part of the Final Solution. Throughout occupied Europe, but most especially in Poland, the

Nazis used ghettos as holding pens where the doomed were assembled to await deportation to a killing center. In a few places, like Lodz, where Morris and his family were confined, the Jews were given a reprieve in order to work for the Nazis. But it was only a reprieve. Death, whether immediate or delayed, was the looming reality of the ghetto.

Although misery was a constant in the Holocaust ghettos, they differed in other ways. The number of people might range from a few Jews in small towns to large numbers in urban areas. The biggest ghettos were in Poland. At its peak population, the largest, Warsaw, held approximately 445,000 people. The second largest, Lodz, held approximately 204,800.[2] The length of time a ghetto existed also varied. Some lasted only the few days or weeks it took to assemble the local Jews. Other ghettos, especially those where the Jews worked in war production, lasted longer. In these, the population included virtually no children or elderly people, since they were deemed nonessential to the labor force and selected early for deportation.

While the SS exercised authority over the ghettos and made all decisions concerning them, a Council of Jews known as the *Judenrat* worked within the ghettos to carry out Nazis orders and organize daily life.[3] The leader of the *Judenrat* was called "Eldest of the Jews" [Ältester]. These councils, modeled after the institutions for self-government which had traditionally existed in the Jewish ghettos, relieved the Germans of the daily work of administration and were an efficient way to maintain order in the ghetto. The councils distributed ration cards and food, set up hospitals, and tried to provide essential services like garbage and sewage collection and disposal of the dead. Included in the SS directives was the task of providing lists of those to be deported and then delivering the victims to the train station. The latter job fell to the Jewish police. That the councils were helpful to the Nazis is a certainty. Whether they betrayed the Jews is a question that persists.

My confinement in a ghetto began in March 1940 in my hometown of Pabianice. Rumors of the Nazis' intention to establish a ghetto had circulated for weeks before the plans were implemented. It was these rumors that caused Father to bring my mom, Bluma, and me back from the little town where he had sent us at the end of 1939.

When the plan was finally announced, the Jews of Pabianice were given twenty-four hours to move into a few square blocks in the "old city," the area where our family lived. In order to squeeze everyone into this space, the Jews who were already living there were required to house those

who were forced to relocate. An older couple and a single woman who was
a dentist were placed with our family. This situation was tolerable, as our
"guests" were quiet, and we rarely saw them. Probably about nine thousand Jews were crammed into the Pabianice ghetto. Had many not previously fled eastward to escape the German occupation, there would have
been more.

Our ghetto was an "open ghetto," which meant that Gentiles could
freely enter and leave it. The Jews, however, were forbidden to leave. Lest
we forget, large signs were posted on the boundaries of the ghetto warning that any Jew caught outside its perimeters would be shot. Because the
ghetto was "open" to Gentiles, our former housekeeper, Steffa, and some
of my father's workers would bring us food, and in exchange, we gave
them fur coats, gold pieces, or whatever else we had. With this extra food
to supplement our rations, things were not too bad, at least not at first. We
had vegetables, potatoes, a little meat, and some bread and margarine.
Mom always made sure that there was food for the "baby," and somehow
she provided me with an egg every day. Of course, we had no chocolate or
sweets—I missed them!

Life continued but it was far from the life we had known before the
occupation. There were no more schools, movies or parks, and there was
a 7 p.m. curfew. Despite these limitations, we did our best to minimize the
dreariness of ghetto life. My friends and I continued to play soccer and
cowboys in the backyard, and the adults tore down the backyard fences and
walls so that they could move around more easily and visit after curfew.

In an effort to seal us off completely from the outside world, radios
were banned in the ghetto, and newspapers were prohibited. For news of
the war, we had to rely on snippets of information that circulated throughout the ghetto. News of the fall of France in the spring of 1940 was simply
devastating; it was terrible, unexpected, and depressing. The invasion of
the Soviet Union in June of 1941 was generally greeted as good news.
My mom, however, was not overly enthusiastic. Remembering how the
Russians had treated civilians in World War I, she feared having them in
Poland again. She said that she would prefer to be liberated by the British
rather than the Russians, even if we had to wait a little longer. Of course,
she could not have foreseen how many years it would be before liberation;
nor could she have imagined how few of her family would still be alive
when that day arrived.

The reports we received suggested that there was little or no chance
that the Soviet army would liberate Poland any time soon or, for that mat-

ter, ever. An acquaintance who had fled to Russia at the time of the invasion but subsequently returned to visit his sick mother gave us disheartening accounts of the Soviet army. He described it as primitive and almost nonfunctional; he said that the soldiers' guns were attached by ropes, not leather. Relief from the East any time soon seemed a fantasy.

One of the few things that brought relief from the bad news about the war and the grimness of my daily life was the Zionist youth meetings. Because Zionist groups were outlawed, the meetings were held in secret, but, at least, I now had my parent's permission to attend. I belonged to the youngest group, and our meetings were held on the top floor of an abandoned factory. So as not to arouse suspicion, we used different entrances and entered singly. As an extra precaution, lookouts were posted. If, despite these measures we were caught, we were to say that we were part of the Jugendpflege [Helping the Youth] organization, which was legal. All of this secrecy was appealing, but the main attraction was the meetings. They functioned as a drug. We sang songs of hope and of liberation, we dreamed about a future in our own state where there would be no persecution, and we fantasized about life in Palestine. Zionist meetings were an antidote to our hopelessness.

Another break from the boredom and dreariness of ghetto life and a further reminder of my Jewishness was the celebration of my bar mitzvah. My family tried to make this occasion as festive as possible. Mom baked something resembling a cake and fixed something like Kool-Aid, and we invited our relatives and a few friends to celebrate. My mom, who was more observant than my dad, wanted me to lay the tefillin [wrap my arms]. When she insisted, Father responded, "Leave the child alone." He very gently reminded her that there was a war going on and that under the circumstances this ritual could be omitted. Ultimately, I was relieved of a duty that I considered to be a nuisance, especially since I was now working and really did not have the time for it.

Despite our attempts to live as normally as possible, life was anything but normal. To begin with I was now working eight to ten hours a day, six days a week, in a factory making hats for German soldiers and civilians. At first I sewed the linings for the hats by hand; later I was assigned to use a specialized sewing machine to make them. I was only twelve, and I was very proud of this promotion. Working at a machine made me feel like an adult. I also was paid for my work but the most important thing about having a job was getting an identification card. Identification cards were highly prized as they provided security from being randomly seized and taken to a work camp. Later, in Lodz, these cards provided temporary immunity from deportation and death.

My brother and sisters also worked. Nachman and Rozka worked in a large factory making uniforms for soldiers and Bluma took care of young children in something like a day-care center. Mom stayed home tending the house and cooking. Performing these tasks without help was a new experience for her, and, although she never complained, I know it was exhausting work.

My dad was responsible for many things in the ghetto. He was in charge of organizing the existing factories and the workers. In addition, he created new factories which enabled more Jews to have that all-important job. One idea that he implemented was using furs that had been seized from Jews to make gloves, ear muffs, and face masks for the German soldiers. Father was also busy as a member of the Jewish Council and then as its leader. Because several of the previous leaders had been sent to prison, Mother considered the position to be bad luck and begged him at least not to take the title of "Eldest." Nevertheless, with or without the title, my father was the leader of the ghetto and a very busy man. Because our family and many members of the Jewish Council lived in our apartment building, it became known as "The House of Lords."

The Jewish police were an essential part of the ghetto government. They maintained order and patrolled the borders of the ghetto to ensure that no one escaped. The police also had the job of supplying people for Germans labor gangs. I remember at least three occasions when the police took large groups out of the Pabianice ghetto, two of men and one of women. At first, some of the Jews who were sent out to work returned, but usually they did not. Later in Lodz, when the Jewish police were used to round up people for deportation, they became the objects of resentment and hatred. But, in Pabianice and in Lodz, I thought that the Jewish police generally buffered us from the even greater brutality we would have suffered from the Nazis. To be sure, the Jewish police were not to be envied.

One of the few humorous stories that I remember from my time in the Pabianice ghetto is about the chief of the police, a man named Kupperwasser. Mr. Kupperwasser lived in our apartment building with the family of my friend Abraham and he stuttered badly. So the story went, a young couple who was very much in love unintentionally wandered outside the ghetto and were caught and imprisoned. Mr. Kupperwasser and the Jewish Council decided to obtain their release, and to this end they collected diamond rings and other valuables that they used successfully as *ransom. When asked how he had obtained the couple's release, the chief supposedly declared, "Youuu jjjust have to kkknow how to ttttalk." For years, that was a favorite story among the survivors of the ghetto.[4]*

Mr. Kupperwasser's stuttering is an isolated humorous anecdote amidst a sea of horrific stories. One terrible incident that I witnessed involved Dr. Wanda Swider, the lady dentist who lived in one of our rooms. Somehow the Kripo *[German criminal police] heard that she had implanted diamonds in people's teeth, and so they took her in for questioning to obtain the names of the people with the diamonds. Dr. Swider was a very heavy woman, and the* Kripo *began the proceedings by making her run around a lumberyard until she fell down. They then beat her until she was close to death. Despite the brutality Dr. Swider would not or could not provide a list. Finally they brought her back to the apartment and warned her that they would question her again during the coming week.*

Dr. Swider's room had a window on the street. Shortly after she returned I heard her scream, "This is the end," and then I heard a loud boom. I ran to a window and saw her body sprawled in the street below. She had cut her wrist and then thrown herself out of the window. When we went into her room, all we found was my sister's watch and a note thanking my sister for having lent it. I was quite young at the time of this incident, but the memory remains fresh.

A few weeks after Dr. Swider's death, the Kripo *came for my father. They knew he was wealthy, and they wanted to know where his valuables were hidden. When my dad returned from being questioned, he was black-and-blue and could scarcely walk. My mom and sisters made compresses and tried as best as they could to relieve his pain. The next day the* Kripo *came again, and this time Father took them to his factory and dug up the valuables that he had hidden. Although we did everything to nurse my father back to health, I don't believe that he ever fully recovered from this beating. It seemed to me that he was never quite the same. As far as I know he showed them everything, but the* Kripo *evidently were not satisfied. When we were in Lodz, they came for him again and beat him again. My father was not the only wealthy Jew to receive this treatment; inquiries about property and beatings were common, especially when we were in Lodz.*

Life in Pabianice could be brutal, but had it not been for Keller, the German official in charge of our ghetto, it might have been much worse. Keller was a huge man whose formidable presence was enhanced by his omnipresent and ominous German shepherd. But appearances can be deceiving—Keller turned out to be a gentle giant much in the mold of Otto Schindler. While it was he who relayed orders from the SS to the Jewish Council, it is believed that he tried to minimize their harshness. It was because of Keller that the Pabianice ghetto remained open enabling us to supplement our meager rations by purchasing food from Polish Gentiles. Unfortunately, Keller was powerless against the Kripo *and the SS.*

We became aware of just how much worse our situation could be in the winter of 1940-1941, when we began to learn about the hunger and even starvation that was ravaging the Lodz ghetto. There, the Nazis deliberately withheld food from the Jews to force them to spend what wealth they had to buy it. In addition, the ghetto was closed, which meant that the Poles were unable to bring food into the ghetto. Responding to stories about the desperate plight of the Lodz Jews, the Jews in Pabianice and other nearby ghettos somehow obtained permission to have potatoes and vegetables delivered to their relatives there. They procured and bundled food which was then transported by Polish farmers into the city. Since almost everyone in the smaller towns had relatives in Lodz, these food deliveries helped many people there. I suspect that they were the difference between life and death for many Lodz Jews. My father was instrumental in making these deliveries happen, and this evidently brought his name to the attention of the leader of the Lodz ghetto, Chaim Rumkowski. Recognition of my father's service would benefit our family when we were sent to Lodz in the summer of 1942.

While our life was restricted, uncomfortable, and occasionally violent, we knew we were at least much better off than the Jews of Lodz. We became acutely aware of this during the winter of 1942 when we started hearing rumors that some of the Lodz Jews were being put on trains, so it was said, to be resettled in the East. The fact that no one ever again saw those who left fortified our gut feeling that this development was not good. The truth is that the trains were headed to a place called Chelmno [Kulmhof in German], which was located about forty miles northwest of Lodz. At Chelmno, the Jews were subsequently gassed.[5] Although I did not learn about Chelmno until I was in Lodz, it is possible that my father already knew about it. So, fearful of the devil we did not know, we were content to remain in our ghetto in Pabianice.

We felt relatively safe there. After all, our factories were busily producing goods for the Germans, and it seemed that our situation would continue for a long time. Unfortunately, this was not to be. On Saturday, May 16, 1942, our life in Pabianice came to an abrupt end when the Nazis liquidated our ghetto. This event marked a turn for the worse in my already miserable existence. It was my initiation into the totality of the horror of the Holocaust.

As I remember, May 16th was a beautiful spring day. The tranquility of the Jewish Sabbath (the Germans seemed deliberately to choose holy days for their worst deeds) was broken when German officials entered our ghetto and announced on loud speakers in both Polish and German that all Jews must assemble in front of their homes at four o'clock. From there we were to march down Warsaw Street to a large soccer field at the edge of the town. We were told not to bring anything. I don't remember how much time there was between the announcement and when we assembled. I do know it must have been short because, when I went to clean the abandoned apartments following the liquidation, there was still food on most tables.

The announcement caught the ghetto by surprise. Usually before the Germans inaugurated some action against us, there were rumors circulating throughout the ghetto. But, we had no foreknowledge of the liquidation. Our ignorance may be explained by the fact that the Pabianice ghetto was the first in the area to be liquidated. As soon as we heard the announcement, an atmosphere of foreboding gripped the ghetto. We knew that nothing good would happen, and our hearts were heavy.

Promptly at four my family gathered in front of our apartment and we began walking toward Warsaw Street. There, we joined a very long line of Jews plodding along on the cobblestone streets next to the trolley tracks. Photographs of the march show a beautiful Warsaw Street lined by leafy trees and punctuated by church steeples.[6] The beauty of the route is in sharp contrast with the solemn line of marching Jews. Photographs of the march show the Jews dressed in heavy coats displaying the Star of David on both the front and the back. The women have on scarves and the men are wearing hats. Some adults carry small bags, and the young people have backpacks. Parents are shown carrying infants and holding the hands of small children. I held the hand of my sister Rozka—I held it very tightly. There is a look of apprehension on the faces of the marchers; no one is smiling. [See the photographs at the end of the chapter.]

I remember it that way, and I also remember things the photographs cannot show. I remember the silence. There was no talking. All you could hear was soft crying and praying. The photographs also show a few Polish people on the sidewalks watching the Jews. The Poles are easy to spot because they are not burdened with stars on their coats. I recall thinking that they seemed happy to see us go, and I remember hearing them mutter things like, "Good riddance" and "Don't come back." My recollection of the Poles' satisfied faces still hurt. That image is impossible for me to forget.

One aspect of the march that seemed strange to me was that there were no SS men along the route—no German uniforms to be seen. Order was maintained by the Jewish police and the local gendarmes. The whereabouts of the SS became apparent when we arrived at the soccer field—there were SS everywhere. I had never seen so many of them, and though my fears undoubtedly exaggerated the number, it seemed to me that there were thousands of SS there.

A number of SS were stationed at the entrance where they were separating the people into different groups and telling them where to go. My family was put in the smallest group by far, a group of 182 people who had been chosen to help clean the ghetto. Another group was made up of healthy people between the ages of roughly 11 and 45; this group was sent to Lodz to work in the factories.[7] A third group consisted of the very young, the elderly and the sick. This group, we learned later, was deported to Chelmno to be killed. A monument commemorating the Jews of Pabianice has been erected there.[8]

A mere description of the groups does not describe the agony that accompanied the selections. Even after the passage of some sixty-five years, it is painful for me to recall the scene; the agony was such that words are inadequate to describe it.

It was terrible—a nightmare, a hell. As I stood in the growing dark, gripping my sister's hand, I watched the SS snatch infants from the arms of their mothers toss them into a pile, a pile that seemed to grow into a mountain as more and more babies were thrown on it. The frantic crying and screaming coming from that pile was echoed by the toddlers and little children whom the SS had herded together, but who were continually breaking away and desperately searching for their parents. At the same time, the mothers clutched their children and screamed, cried, begged, and prayed. Despite being repeatedly beaten, they refused to part with their children. I watched an SS man fling a baby against a concrete wall as a warning to the mothers. I had never seen brutality like this. I simply could not believe what I was seeing.[9]

This agony went on for hours and hours, and we stood and we watched. I knew that I was there. But I kept thinking that it wasn't really happening, that I would awaken, and it would have all been a bad dream. I had never seen and I could never have imagined anything like the grim frenzy and crushing grief of that night. I was never again to see anything as terrible—and I observed many horrible things. After what seemed like an eternity, the day grew darker and darker, and the moaning and wailing became more and more muted. By the time we left the field, it was very quiet.

At some point trucks removed both those Jews going to Chelmno and those going to Lodz. Very late in the evening, our small group trudged back to Pabianice. Among those in our group was Nonek, Bluma's boyfriend and the elder brother of my friend Abraham. Originally Nonek had not been assigned to our group, but when one of the men left it to join his family, Bluma pulled Nonek in to fill the vacant place. I mention this because later in Auschwitz, Nonek would save my life. Also included in our group were father's uncle Bernard and his son Max.[10]

As far as I know, except for Bernard and Max, none of our relatives who were then living in the Pabianice ghetto survived the selection. We know that father's sister Bleema and her husband were among those sent to Chelmno. We assume that their four children, son-in-law, and three grandchildren were also among those gassed there, as we never heard of them again. No one in my mother's family survived the selection—at least we never saw or heard of any of them again. Mother's family included her brother Moshe and his wife (their daughter, Esther, had already fled eastward), her sister Chuma and her husband and three children, and her sister Bronia and her husband and three children. They all perished.

Before I complete my recollections of May 16, I want to recount two incidents that shed light on both the heroism and the helplessness of the Jews. On a day when the SS abundantly displayed the depths of human cruelty, the actions of one Jew, Motush Chmura, served to remind us that man is indeed a noble creature capable of selflessness and bravery. Even before the liquidation, Motush was well known in the ghetto for his compassion and courage. He earned this reputation when, as one of the leaders of the Jewish Council, he was imprisoned for distributing the ration cards of deceased Jews to the living who did not have them. When he was released from prison a few months later, he was welcomed as a hero in the ghetto. I later learned that on the night of the selections, Motush volunteered to accompany the doomed children. Although I did not actually see them depart, the story has been confirmed by his daughter, my friend Helen Chmura Aronson. In a short article that Helen wrote about her experiences in the Holocaust, she states that her father was singing the "Hatikvah" the Jewish anthem, when he accompanied the children to their death.[11]

If Motush's choice of dying with the children illustrates one man's nobility when confronted with the brutality of the Final Solution, the story of what happened to another Jew, Hilet Finkelstein, helps to demonstrate just how limited were the possible responses of the Jews to Nazi oppression. Hilet lived near us; he was friend of mine and a fine athlete. On hearing the order for the Jews to assemble, he decided to escape by climbing out of the window of an apartment on the border of the ghetto. As he was walking away from the ghetto, a Pole spotted him and informed a policeman. Hilet was promptly arrested and shot on the spot. News of his death spread rapidly, so I knew about it before the march began. Without a doubt, Hilet's fate intimidated the other Jews and compelled their obedience to the Nazis' orders. I was to become very familiar with the Nazis' coercive tactics in Lodz and in the camps.

Hilet Finkelstein's story partially answers a question that people often ask: "Why didn't you flee or defend yourself." I find this an easy question to answer. First, there was no place for us to go and no one to help us. This was especially true in my area of Poland where the land was flat and where there were many Germans among the population. Second, for millennia we had been told not to resist and, furthermore, Nazi retaliation to resistance was brutal and often collective. Third, we were weak from hunger and malnutrition and we had no weapons. Last, we always were hoping that our situation would change for the better. The Nazis intentionally and diligently fostered this hope.

After the SS had completed the selections, those 182 of us who had been chosen to stay and clean the ghetto were marched to a factory, where we spent the night. It was late when we arrived, and we were all exhausted. I don't believe that any of us slept—I know I didn't. I kept rerunning the events of the day over and over in my mind in an effort to understand them. So much had happened in the preceding hours—it was simply too much to comprehend. While the events of that day are indelibly stamped in my memory, I still cannot fully understand what happened. Somehow the night passed and morning came, and we began the routine that we would follow during the months it took to complete cleaning the ghetto.

The cleanup crew included people of different professions—tailors, cobblers, doctors, dentists, plumbers, teamsters, and assorted other workers. We assembled every morning and were counted and given our orders for that day. During the day we went about our separate jobs. In the evening, we reassembled, and were counted again, and we reported what we had accomplished. My job and that of most of the group was to take potentially useful items from the homes of the departed Jews and deliver them to a warehouse for sorting. The Germans then took everything away in trucks, presumably to be shipped back to Germany. You have to admit that the Germans were resourceful. They found a use for everything and nothing was wasted. Fortunately for us, Mr. Keller was the German official in charge of the operation. Once again, my father was very busy. He and a younger man were in charge of the workers and kept the records.

Among those who were part of the group was the father of my good friend, Gershon Litmanowicz. Gershon's father was an excellent tailor, and he continued, as he had before the liquidation, to work outside the ghetto making clothes for the SS and their families. One day an SS officer kicked him very hard at the base of his spine. Mr. Litmanowicz never recovered and he died in Lodz within the year. Other than this act, our stay during the clean-up was relatively free of violence.

I mention Gershon not only because of the treatment his father received but also as a way of introducing my only close friend to have survived the Holocaust. As of this writing, Gershon is still alive, and I often visit him in Israel. He is my main connection with the past. Gershon is the only member of his immediate family to have survived. As with most survivors, he does not know where the remains of his mother and brother are located. However, since his father died in Lodz while the dead were still being buried in individual, marked graves, Gershon visits his father's grave whenever possible. In this, he is fortunate.

After three months our work was nearing completion. The cleanup had not been that taxing, the food wasn't too bad, and the conditions were tolerable. Compared to what awaited us in Lodz, it had not been a bad three months. The move to Lodz came suddenly. One day in August, we were told to prepare to leave Pabianice, and within two hours we were loaded onto trucks and transported to the bigger and grimmer Lodz ghetto. I wore four layers of clothing, and I crammed everything I could into my backpack. Yet, nothing I could have done would have prepared me for the Lodz ghetto. I was fourteen.

1. Morris's observation about deaths in the ghettos is corroborated by Hilberg, *The Destruction of the European Jews*, 3:1320.

   TABLE B-1, DEATHS BY CAUSE

   Ghettoization and general privation ....over 800,000
         Ghettos in German-occupied Eastern Europe.............over 600,000
         Theresienstadt and privation outside of ghettos...................100,000
         Transnistria colonies (Romanian and Soviet Jews).............100,000

Writing specifically about deaths in the Lodz ghetto, David Crowe states, "Twenty-one percent would die of typhus and other diseases associated with crowded living conditions and malnutrition." Crowe, *The Holocaust*, 173.

2. Crowe, *The Holocaust*, 173 and 176. This number for Lodz reflects only the Jewish population. Later in the same book, Crowe notes (175-176) that in November 1941 almost 5,000 Roma (Gypsies) were sent to the Lodz ghetto. Shortly thereafter they were deported to Chelmno where they were gassed.

3. Most Jewish Councils were called the *Jüdenrate*; however, in Lodz it was called the *Ältestenrat*.

4. When I asked Morris how many Jews from Pabianice survived, he replied, "Hard to say. Of the 9,000 in the ghetto maybe 1,000 survived. There was a society of the Pabianice survivors; in the 50s and 60s we had a few hundred members."

5. Chelmno [Kulmhof] was built specifically to kill the Jews in Lodz and the surrounding area. It opened in December 1941, and it was the first killing center to be operational. At Chelmno, the victims were shoved into vans, where they were asphyxiated by carbon monoxide gas. The bodies were then driven several miles to a wooded area where they were dumped into pits. Toward the end of the war, the bodies were exhumed and burned in an effort to hide the evidence of the murders.

   Crowe, *The Holocaust*, 174, states, "Between January and May, 1942, the Germans, as part of the early stages of the Final Solution, deported 55,000 Jews and 5,000 Roma [Gypsies] from the ghetto to Chelmno. They deported another 20,000 Jews to the death camp in September. These were the last major deportations until the summer of 1944."

6. Roman Peska, *They Were Doomed To Death*, the Jews of Pabianice, 1794-1998 (Pabianice, Poland,1999), www.zchor.org/pabianice/peska.htm (accessed September 28, 2010). Peska's book has not been translated into English. This site has six photographs showing the Jews of Pabianice on their way to the selection on May 16, 1942.

7. Dawid Sierakowiak, *The Diary of Dawid Sierakowiak: Five Notebooks from the Lodz Ghetto*, ed. Alan Adelson, trans. Kamil Turowski (Oxford: Oxford University Press, 1996), 169. In his diary entry for May 19, Dawid notes that the Jews from Pabianice have been "divided into two categories: able vs. unable to work. Only those able to work were sent here."

8. "We Remember Pabianice!," http://www.zchor.org/pabianice/pabianice.htm (accessed September 28, 2010). This site has a picture of the memorial at Chelmno honoring the Jews of Pabianice. It also includes a map of the area, population figures for the Jews of Pabianice from 1793 to 1939, and information about Peska's book, *They Were Doomed To Death, the Jews of Pabianice*.

9. Sierakowiak, *(Lodz) Diary*, 169-170. In his entry for May 20, Dawid writes, "The Pabianice Jews also know nothing about their elderly, their sick, and their children. Children were torn away from their mothers in the most brutal way."

10. "After we had finished the cleanup of the Pabianice ghetto and were sent to Lodz, I do not remember ever seeing Uncle Bernard or Max again. I heard from a friend who was with Max in the camps that he died a day or two after liberation probably from problems connected with eating. Whether Uncle Bernard died in Lodz or did not survive the selection at Auschwitz, I just don't know." Morris Glass

11. Helen Chmura Aronson, "Surviving the Holocaust," in *A Time to Share: Powerful Personal Stories for Teaching History and Citizenship*, ed. David Savill with Bernie Arigho, Pam Schweitzer, and Clare Summerskill (London: An Age Exchange Publication, London, 2002), 24-29. Helen, Morris' friend, recounts that Rumkowski, the leader of the Lodz ghetto, took her, her mom, and her brother under his wing as a result of her father's act of compassion. When Lodz was liquidated in August 1944, Helen hid in an underground bunker. She was subsequently liberated by the Russians.

Day of the liquidation of the Pabianice ghetto, May 16, 1942. Jews leaving the ghetto and entering Warsaw Street. At the corner is a rectangular sign with the Star of David which marks the boundary of the ghetto.

Jews marching down Warsaw Street on the day that the Pabianice ghetto
was liquidated, May 16, 1942.

Jews marching down Warsaw Street on the day that the Pabianice ghetto
was liquidated, May 16, 1942.

Chapter 7

Jewish Ghettos:
A History and Description

From August 1942, when we were transported from Pabianice, until August 1944, when we were deported to Auschwitz, my family and I were imprisoned in the Lodz ghetto. Horrible as our previous experiences had been, we were unprepared for the grimness of life in Lodz. It was a life of exhausting work, filth, cold, hunger, fear, and death. It was a nightmare from which one did not awake. Despite the bleakness of our situation, my family and I managed to survive. We were fortunate to have each other. Having the love and understanding of my family sustained me. It gave me hope and courage. It gave me a reason to survive no matter how hungry or cold or weary I was. Without the comfort of my family, I would have been overwhelmed by the wretchedness that enveloped me when I entered Lodz. Morris Glass

The Lodz ghetto existed from April 1940 until August 1944. It was the first major Holocaust ghetto to be opened, and it was the last to be liquidated. In between these dates, an epic story of a doomed people's struggle to survive unspeakable conditions, exhausting work, and death by starvation, disease, or deportation to a killing center unfolded. It was a story in which false hopes fostered by the oppressors sustained the oppressed. We know what the Jews either did not know or chose not to acknowledge—all were doomed. Their attempt to save themselves by working hard was in vain;

the only ones rewarded by their efforts were the Germans, who prospered from the output of the ghetto industries. The Jewish workers, no matter how productive or how essential their contribution, would die; no other outcome was possible.

Numerous sources about the Lodz ghetto are available. Records compiled by the Jewish administrators in the ghetto, contemporary diaries written by ghetto dwellers, and a chronicle of the ghetto written and buried by Jewish archivists furnish a wealth of material about life there. These sources are augmented by photographs taken illegally by Jews, drawings depicting ghetto life, artifacts like ghetto money and stamps, and by accounts written by survivors—there were probably more survivors of Lodz than any other major ghetto. Furthermore, the Germans departed in a hurry, thus leaving many of their records intact. The Germans also made films of the ghetto, some of which were incorporated into *The Eternal Jew*, a widely available Nazi propaganda film.[1]

The distinctiveness of the Lodz ghetto was due in large part to the geography of the city. A major industrial center and the second most populous city in Poland, Lodz is located in the western part of the country in close proximity to Germany. This closeness to Germany affected developments in the ghetto in a number of ways. In particular, it partially explains why this ghetto lasted so long. Location determined that Lodz would be occupied shortly after the Germans invaded Poland in September 1939, and that it would not be in the path of the Soviet offensive until fairly late in the war. Thus the Lodz ghetto was among the first ghettos to be created and the last to be liquidated.

Another key ingredient to the longevity of the ghetto was its industrial capacity. Like Manchester, England, a city to which it is often compared, Lodz was a product of the Industrial Revolution. It was the center of textile production in eastern Europe. It was the possibility of exploiting her factories and trained labor force that made Lodz an obvious choice as a manufacturing center for armaments, uniforms, and other commodities that were essential to the German war effort. And it was the output of her factories that caused the Germans to postpone the final liquidation of the ghetto until the last summer of the war.

Lodz's proximity to Germany, along with the economic opportunities its industries afforded, attracted a large number of Germans to live and work there. In 1931, about 9 percent of the population was of German origin; these people were known as *Volksdeutsche* [Germans living outside of Germany].[2] After the Nazis occupied the city, they intentionally sought to increase the number of Germans as part of their effort to "Aryanize" the area. In fact, the Nazis chose Lodz to be a showplace of German superiority, a Nazi "city on a hill" that would be a model for the Germanized eastern Europe that they envisioned in the future. As a result, Lodz became two cities—the Jewish ghetto, an island of unbelievable squalor, and the surrounding city, an increasingly Germanized and modernized place. Besides giving the Nazis an established base of support, the large number of Germans in Lodz would have made it more difficult for the Jews to resist the Nazis and to escape from the ghetto. It also undoubtedly facilitated the Nazis' efforts to isolate the Lodz ghetto from news about the war and from contacts with Poles, resistance groups, and other ghettos.

The topography of the area also discouraged flight from the Lodz ghetto. Located on the Great European Plain in an area of fairly flat land and few forests, the natural environment of western Poland was not one that nurtured hiding. Furthermore, there was no place to flee. Unlike areas in eastern Poland that afforded escape into unoccupied territory, Lodz was surrounded by German-controlled lands. Thus, the options of the Lodz Jews were limited by both a hostile population and by geography.

In addition to the *Volksdeutsche* who lived in the area, Lodz and the towns surrounding it were home to a large Jewish population. At the time of the German invasion, Lodz had approximately 600,000 inhabitants of whom about 223,000, or 32 percent, were Jewish.[3] Only Warsaw had a larger Jewish population (368,000 Jews out of a total population of 1,260,000). Lodz was surrounded by a number of smaller towns that were economically and socially connected to it. Morris's hometown of Pabianice was among them. Many of the Jewish inhabitants of these towns, like Morris's family, were sent to the Lodz ghetto. Most of those who were not sent to Lodz were deported to Chelmno, a killing center located some 40 miles northwest of Lodz that was built expressly to murder the Jews of Lodz and its neighboring towns. Chelmno was the first killing center to be operational; it began gassing Jews in December 1941.

Although the mass killings at Chelmno did not begin until over two years after the Germans occupied the area, other changes were inaugurated almost immediately. Shortly after entering Lodz, the Nazis incorporated it and the western areas of Poland directly into the Third Reich [literally, the Third State—the term refers specifically to the Nazi state]. The area was immediately subjected to intensive Germanization. Streets were renamed after notable Nazis, and German was proclaimed the official language. By the spring of 1940, the name of the city had been changed to Litzmannstadt in honor of a German general in World War I. The Nazis also encouraged the local Gentile population to harass and humiliate the Jews, to loot and destroy Jewish shops and businesses, and to destroy synagogues. So that they could easily be identified, in November it was decreed that all Jews must wear the Star of David on the front and the back of their clothing. As a result of this early persecution, many thousands of Jews fled from Lodz.

It appears that plans for a ghetto were set in motion in late 1939 and early 1940. Early in January, using the false claim that an outbreak of disease among the Jews necessitated separating them from the Gentile population (this claim was used in other cities as well), the Germans announced that all the Jews were to move into a designated area. This directive also meant also that the Gentiles living there must leave. Perceiving that the Jews were procrastinating, the Germans murdered hundreds of them in early March to hasten the move into the ghetto. While the Jews were moving in, the Germans were constructing a barbed-wire fence around the ghetto. This fence was completed on April 30, and on May 1, the Lodz ghetto became the first "closed" ghetto, an area sealed off from the rest of the world. Jews could not leave it, and Gentiles could not enter it. Throughout its existence, Lodz remained a tightly sealed community—perhaps the most tightly sealed of all the major ghettos.[4]

The ghetto occupied about four square kilometers within the city of Lodz and some of the city's major streets ran through it. Preventing contact between the Jews who lived in the ghetto and the Gentiles who used these streets was a problem. The solution was to surround the streets with fences and then to construct footbridges across them for the Jews to use. This arrangement allowed the Gentiles to traverse these streets in trucks, cars, and trolleys, while at the same time, it also revealed to them the true nature of ghetto life. The footbridges spanning the ghetto streets became one of the most visible symbols of the isolation and subjugation of the Lodz Jews. It would have been impossible for anyone in Lodz to maintain ignorance about the condition of the Jews in the ghetto.

The number of Jews in the ghetto fluctuated. About 167,000 Jews from Lodz were crammed into the ghetto when it was closed in the spring of 1940. In the next two years approximately 40,000 Jews from the surrounding area and from Germany, Austria, Luxembourg and Czechoslovakia were brought to Lodz. It is estimated that a minimum of 200,000 Jews were forced into the ghetto during its existence. In addition, about 5,000 Gypsies were sent there.[5]

At the same time that new Jews were being forced into the ghetto, the Jews already there were dying or being deported to the killing centers. The death rate within the Lodz ghetto was the highest of any major ghetto. Between 1940 and 1944, at least 20 percent of the original ghetto population, over 40,000 Jews, died of starvation, disease, or freezing.[6] As these figures suggest, the living conditions were primitive, unsanitary, and horrible. Most of the ghetto dwellings had no running water. There was no modern sewage system— only outhouses—and there was little coal or wood for heat. The most pressing problem in the ghetto, however, was the scarcity of food. Hunger was a constant.[7] The theme of hunger dominates Morris's recollections and those of other Jews, and it is also the dominant theme of the so-called "street songs" of the ghetto.[8]

The high number of deaths among the Lodz Jews reflects the longevity of the ghetto as well as its miserable living conditions. The ghetto lasted so many years that Jews often died there before the Nazis deported them. In fact, the situation in other ghettos may have been worse.

Everything else in the ghetto was under the control of the Nazis. Nothing went into or out of the ghetto and nothing happened within the ghetto without their approval. From the beginning the Germans cultivated the notion that the ghetto was autonomous by establishing a Jewish Council, the *Ältestenrat* [Council of Elders], and by appointing a Jewish leader for the ghetto.[9] But self-rule was always an illusion. Another illusion the Nazis fostered was that working hard to produce war materials for Germany would ensure the Jews survived. The leader of the ghetto, Chaim Rumkowski, enthusiastically supported this idea.

Chaim Rumkowski (1877-1944) was probably the most controversial Jewish figure to emerge during the Holocaust. Many consider him to have been a tyrant who partnered with the Nazis in exploiting and deporting the Jews. Others believe that by helping to make the ghetto productive, he delayed the final deportations and thus increased the possibility of surviving. Indeed, this argument may explain why there were probably more survivors of Lodz than of any major ghetto. Most agree that Rumkowski ruled the ghetto with an iron hand, that he had an elevated opinion of himself, and that he had a talent for organization and administration. He was known as "the King."

To his credit, under Rumkowski's leadership a population of almost two hundred thousand people was housed, fed, employed, and kept in order. No opposition to his rule was permitted—prison or death awaited those who protested or conspired against him. Those who worked closely with Rumkowski and supported him were rewarded or, to use the ghetto word, "protected." They received better accommodations and more food, and they and their families were exempt from the early deportations. Among those chosen for better treatment were the Jewish police, who had the unenviable job of filling the trains headed for the killing centers. But deportation was a reality, a reality which would ultimately embrace both the Jewish police and Rumkowski.

Deportations from Lodz began in December 1941 and ended with the liquidation of the ghetto in August 1944. (Morris and his family were among the last to be deported.) Throughout most of the ghetto's existence, the Lodz Jews were shipped some 40 miles to Chelmno to be gassed in vans and dumped into pits in the forest. Not until the summer of 1944 were they deported to Auschwitz. At first, most of those selected for deportation and death were Jews from western European countries who had been brought into Lodz, Gypsies, criminals, and those unable to work. It is estimated that between December 1941 and December 1942, over 70,000 Jews from Lodz and the surrounding towns and 5,000 Gypsies were murdered at Chelmno.[10]

The deportations that are seared into the minds of those who witnessed them occurred during eight days in September 1942. The prelude to these deportations began with an announcement on September 4 that everyone in the ghetto was to assemble at the main square to hear a pronouncement by Rumkowski. In a well-documented speech, Rumkowski announced that the SS had demanded the deportation of twenty-thousand persons. Imploring, "Fathers, mothers give me your children," Rumkowski announced that all children under ten and the old and sick must be given over to the Germans for deportation.[11] This announcement was followed by eight days of absolute terror during which the Jewish police, accompanied by the SS, selected the candidates for death. Each day, everyone had to stand outside of his dwelling until all the selections had been made. The eight days came to be known as the "*Gehsperre*" [Curfew] because the Jews were put under a strict curfew to curtail movement within the ghetto.

Following the *Gehsperre*, major deportations from Lodz ceased until the summer of 1944. During this year-and-a-half interlude, Lodz was truly a Nazi workshop, a slave labor camp that fueled the Nazi war machine. All buildings, including those that had previously been used as orphanages, schools, and hospitals were now factories. The only people who remained in the ghetto were those who could work. During this time, it appeared that a remnant of the Lodz Jews just might survive by making themselves indispensable to the Nazis.

But that was not to be. By the beginning of 1944, with the German army in retreat, the Nazis decided to move quickly to murder any Jews remaining within their reach. In early June, Heinrich Himmler, the man in charge of the Final Solution, decreed that the Lodz ghetto would be closed and its Jews deported. Between June 23 and August 23, about 75,000 Jews left Lodz for the killing centers, and the Lodz ghetto ceased to exist. Some 877 Jews, most of whom survived by hiding from the Germans, remained behind to clean up the ghetto. They were liberated by the Russians in January 1945. Of those who were sent to Chelmno in the summer of 1944, it appears that the only survivor was a young boy, Simon Srebnik, who was shot and left for dead.[12] Of those sent to Auschwitz, it is estimated that two-thirds were selected for death. Probably between 7,000 and 10,000 of the Jews who had been in the Lodz ghetto, or about 5 percent, survived to the end of the war.[13]

1. "No ghetto left more documentation: official German archives, administrative ghetto records, contemporaneous diaries. The Germans left Lodz in a hurry and had little time to destroy their records. Jewish archivists and chroniclers also buried a great deal of material, including the amazing *Chronicle of the Lodz Ghetto*. And since it was the last ghetto to suffer liquidation, more Jews survived to write memoirs than anywhere else." Samuel D. Kassow, "A Tale of Two Cities," a review of *Ghettostadt: Lodz and the Making of a Nazi City*, by Gordon J. Horwitz, *The New Republic*, (Wednesday, May, 2009), www.tnr.com/articles/books?page=3 (accessed October 17, 2010).

2. Gordon J. Horwitz, *Ghettostadt: Lodz and the Making of a Nazi City* (Cambridge, MA, Harvard University Press, 2008), 3.

3. Crowe, *Holocaust*, 172 and 176. Crowe states that when the Lodz ghetto was sealed in late April only about 162,000 to 164,000 Jews were still there. This means that many thousands had already fled.

4. Lucy Dawidowicz, *The War Against the Jews*, 1933-1945 (New York: Bantam Books, 1986), 205-06. "Warsaw and Lodz, with the largest Jewish populations, were the most tightly, almost hermetically sealed ghettos."

5. USHMM , "Lodz," *Holocaust Encyclopedia*, http://www.ushmm.org/wlc/en/article.php?ModuleId=10005071 (accessed on October 17, 2010). The other sources that I have consulted are in general agreement as to these figures.

6. The figures on deaths within the ghetto vary slightly. "Lodz," *Holocaust Encyclopedia*, states that more than 20 percent of the ghetto's population died as a direct result of the harsh living conditions. Other sources are in close agreement.

   Kassow in his review of *Ghettostadt* states, "About 200,000 Jews passed through the Lodz ghetto. Of these, 43,743 died of sickness and hunger. Kassow, "A Tale," *New Republic*.

7. It is difficult to generalize about the amount of food allotted to each person in the Lodz ghetto. Hilberg, *Destruction*, 1:265 states that for a seven-month period in 1941, that the average monthly allotment for each person was 11/2 pounds of meat, 1 egg, and 12 pounds of potatoes. He also states (1:268) that in April of 1943, the Nazi official in charge of the ghetto wrote to his superior that the food supply in the ghetto was so low that he could no longer guarantee that the workers could continue production. He said that they had had no butter, margarine, or milk and that no fat or potatoes had been added to the soup, which was made with vegetables of poor quality. In *(Lodz) Diary*, Sierakowiak talks constantly about food and hunger.

8. Gila Flam. *Singing for Survival: Songs of the Lodz Ghetto*, 1940-1945 (Urbana: University of Illinois Press, 1992).

9. The Jewish Councils or Council of Elders were commonly referred to as the Judenraete (plural) or Judenrat (singular). However, in Lodz and a few other ghettos, the term used was Ältestenrat.

10. USHMM, "Lodz," *Holocaust Encyclopedia*, January 1942, http://www.ushmm. org/wlc/en/article.php?ModuleId=10005071 (accessed on October 17, 2010).

   Operations at Chelmno halted in March, 1943 and then resumed briefly in the summer of 1944, when 3,000 Jews from Lodz were sent there. In total, approximately 150,000 persons were killed at Chelmno. (Hilberg, *Destruction*, 3:1320.)

11. Chaim Rumkowski, "Rumkowski's Address at the Time of the Deportation of the Children from the Lodz Ghetto, September 4, 1942," in Botwinick, *A Holocaust Reader*, 150.

12. A handful of Jews escaped from Chelmno when it was in operation from 1941-1943. It appears that only one of them, Mordechai Podchlebnik, survived the Holocaust. He testified at the trial of Adolph Eichmann.

13. Kassow, *"A Tale," New Republic*. "Sixty-seven thousand were sent to Auschwitz in August 1944. At that late date, about one in three Jews was selected for forced labor, while the rest were gassed. All in all, about seven thousand to ten thousand survived."

Chapter 8

My Life in the Lodz Ghetto

I could not believe the sights and smells that greeted me when I reached the Lodz ghetto in August 1942. It was like something out of a science-fiction book. It was worlds away from the Pabianice ghetto, and it was horrible beyond my ability to describe it.

As we approached the ghetto, I could smell it—the stench was horrible. On entering, I saw dilapidated buildings, neglected pavements, flooded gutters, and crowded, narrow streets. I saw a barbed-wire fence topped by electric wires, and it had German guards stationed every hundred meters or so along it. I saw traffic moving on a street that was enclosed with barbed wire, and I saw a footbridge connecting the two sides of the street. Now I knew firsthand what a "closed" ghetto was. Most startling of all were the people—they looked like walking death. The expressions on their faces were entirely different from any I had ever seen. It was as though they were not even human.

We had heard that conditions were bad in Lodz but we had no appreciation of just how bad things really were. I immediately knew that life here would be much worse than it had been in Pabianice, that we were entering a different and far grimmer landscape. This was the place that would be my home for the next two years. In contrast, the Pabianice ghetto seemed like Paradise.

My first impressions were supplemented later by images that are seared in my memory. Foremost among these is the image of people pulling carts full of sewage. The faces and clothing of these people still haunt me. Their clothes were rags, and their faces bore the mask of death. And the smell was overwhelming in its awfulness. It is simply impossible to describe. Men, women, and children desperate for food pulled these carts to receive an extra ration of bread. I still remember the children moaning, "Mama, Mama." Starvation is indeed a harsh master!

I also remember children in rags begging in the streets, and dead bodies lying on the sidewalks and in the gutters. The bodies were mere skeletons, and they were usually naked because others, desperate for warmth, stole the clothes. The bodies were picked up and thrown into carts that were drawn by humans, and carried to a communal grave where they were dumped.

Later I also would become aware of what I did not see. There were few children or elderly people—it was a city of workers. There were no flowers, bushes, or trees. All available land was used to grow food. When there was a yard connected to an apartment, it was divided among the occupants who carefully coaxed vegetables from their small holdings. These little plots were precious; stealing from one meant time in prison. All of these images and more were to become an intimate part of my life in Lodz. But on the day of our arrival, my first impressions were crowded out by the appearance of the "King," ghetto leader, Chaim Rumkowski, who came to greet our little group.

As soon as we entered the ghetto, we were taken to a room in Czarnieckiego, the ghetto prison. It was here that I first saw Rumkowski. Overwhelmed as I was by the move from Pabianice to Lodz, I can still remember my first impressions. He was a striking man, tall with a mane of white hair and dark-rimmed glasses. He must have been in his late sixties then, but he looked younger. Furthermore, especially in contrast to the other people whom I had seen in the ghetto, he looked healthy, well fed, and well dressed. I would see him many more times, especially as he rode through the ghetto in his carriage attended by his retinue of lackeys. People, looking for favors, would flock around him.

Whatever less-than-favorable opinions I may have developed later, on that first day Rumkowski proved to be my family's friend. Shortly after meeting Father, Rumkowski inquired where we would like to live and Father replied that we would like to live close to my mom's sister. Rumkowski arranged for us to be placed in the same apartment building. He then asked what job my father would like. Father replied that he wanted a quiet job, one without the decision making and responsibility that he had shouldered in Pabianice. *Rumkowski arranged for Father to work where the clothes of those who had been murdered in the killing centers were sorted. It was an easy job and one which had the added advantage of providing our family with good clothes. I can only surmise as to why Rumkowski singled my father out for special treatment. I believe it was his way of expressing gratitude for the efforts that Father had made to have vegetables and potatoes sent into the Lodz ghetto during the winter of 1940-1941.*

We were not the only family from Pabianice that Rumkowski designated for special treatment. Because of the heroism of Motush Chmura, the man who had volunteered to accompany the children on the day that the Pabianice ghetto was liquidated, Rumkowski also took the Chmura family under his wing.

The help that Rumkowski gave to us and the Chmuras illustrates the meaning of that all important word—"protekcia." Protekcia meant that you had connections with someone in authority who might help you obtain more food, avoid standing in line for rations, get a better job or apartment, and, of greatest importance, avoid being deported. Having protekcia made life much easier and more secure; it was a buffer against the worst aspects of ghetto life. People would talk and brag about their association with anyone who had influence. Wherever you went or whatever you did, you always looked for someone who was in a position to help you, to furnish protekcia.

Because Father had had an office in Lodz before the war, he knew quite a few people who were now in positions of authority in the ghetto. He had a cousin and a number of friends on the Ältestenrat [Council of Elders or Advisory Council], *and he knew other people with important jobs. My sister Rozka also knew some people in Lodz because she had attended high school there. Although I was too young to understand clearly how protekcia worked, as our first meeting with Rumkowski illustrates, there is no doubt that it existed. It is correct to say that there were two groups in the ghetto—those with protekcia and those without. In particular those people on the Advisory Council or those employed by the ghetto administration lived relatively well in comparison with the rest of the people. It was not a fair system, but it was a fact of ghetto life. It was a system that bred resentment and hostility among those who were left out.[1] While we were not among the ghetto elite, the protekcia given us by Rumkowski and others helped shape the context of our life in Lodz. It undoubtedly made our lives marginally less grim.*

While protekcia impacted our family's situation, it was the Gehsperre that shaped our lives and the character of the Lodz ghetto more than anything else that happened during the two years we were imprisoned there. The Gehsperre [German for curfew] *involved the selection and deportation of some twenty thousand children, elderly, and sick. It occurred between September 5 and 12, 1942— about a month after we came to Lodz. Without a doubt, the Gehsperre constituted the single most horrific event in the sad history of the ghetto.*

The Gehsperre began when Rumkowski announced that the Germans had demanded that twenty thousand Jews be deported. Those designated were children under ten, the elderly, and the sick. Neither I nor any of my family was present for the announcement. However, from what we learned from those who were there, Rumkowski made it clear as to what would be the fate of those who were deported. Everyone who heard the speech was moved. We were told that Rumkowski was very emotional, that he spoke as a caring individual, and that he spoke from his heart.[2]

The announcement was followed by eight days of agony and terror as the selections were made and the victims deported. No one went to work. Every day we were forced to stand in a line in front of our apartments until the selections had been completed. Anyone found inside a building was shot. Grouped in families, we stood silently, prayed, and waited for the arrival of the SS and the Jewish police. When they approached, we stood very still. I held my breath and looked straight ahead. I was terrified that I would do something to attract attention to myself. The SS would look up and down the rows of Jews and then they would point at a person or persons to come forward.

Many terrible scenes took place during the Gehsperre—it was awful. When a child was selected, the parents would fall on their knees, clutch the child, cry, beg, and plead. The SS would respond by kicking, beating, or even shooting the mothers and fathers. If a child refused to come forward, the child was shot. In an effort to minimize the brutality, the Jewish police tried to hold the parents back and to keep them from running after their children. A similar scenario occurred when an elderly person was selected. The elderly knew that they were going to their deaths—I heard some of them repeating the shema [last prayers] as they were led away. It was heartbreaking; it was unbearable.

Although several people were taken from our building, my family and my aunt's family were spared. My parents did what they could to look younger. My father shaved his beard and my mother and my aunt rubbed red beets on their cheeks to give color to their faces. What I suspect really saved us was our ages and the fact that we were relatively healthy.

Horrible as the Gehsperre was, it did not have as devastating an impact on me as the liquidation of Pabianice. Perhaps this is because we had just arrived in Lodz, and so I did not know very many people. In contrast, in Pabianice, I knew a lot of people, and so what happened there touched me in a very personal way. Another difference was that in Lodz we understood what was happening; the irrational at least seemed to have some logic. In Pabianice we had had no warning and no explanation. What happened appeared to be totally random and chaotic. Also, sad to say, I may simply have become desensitized to suffering.

The Gehsperre transformed Lodz. It was no longer simply a place where Jews were segregated while awaiting deportation. It had become something more specialized—a slave camp where everyone worked for the German until they were deported and murdered. This transformation of the ghetto shaped our daily lives. We were now not just Jews—we were working Jews. It appeared that as long as we worked, we would live; at least, this was the fiction that the Germans carefully cultivated and that we greedily swallowed.

And so after the Gehsperre we settled into a daily life of hard work and hoped that by working we could survive. At first, we were wary of what might happen next. However, as the deportations became more infrequent and then virtually stopped, we became almost complacent. We developed a feeling that our lives would continue in this mode until somehow we were liberated. But it was not to be. The decision to destroy all the Jews under Nazi control had been made. We had simply been granted a reprieve in order to serve the interests of the Third Reich.

If protekcia impacted our family in small ways, and the Gehsperre transformed the ghetto as a whole, it was our German masters who ultimately determined our fate. The Lodz ghetto was under the control of the SS, and the SS officer in charge was Hans Biebow. I saw him on several occasions. He was an attractive, Germanic-looking man who, so I have been told, made a fortune from the ghetto industries. A story circulated in the ghetto about a friend of Biebow's who told him that he had never seen a Jew, and so Biebow invited him to Lodz. According to the story, when the man looked through the barbed wire fence into the ghetto, he was surprised by what he saw and exclaimed, "Why they aren't Jews, they are human beings." Unfortunately, Biebow did not share his friend's feelings.[3]

Although Biebow was often present in the ghetto, most daily concerns

*were the responsibility of Rumkowski and the Jewish administrators who
functioned as a puppet government for the Germans. It has been affirmed
by many survivors that Rumkowski was a dictator who brooked no opposition, and that the Jewish council functioned as a rubber stamp and did
whatever the "King" said. The bureaucracy that he established was unbelievable—there were ministers for this and ministers for that, and they kept
records of everything. They knew where you lived and where you worked.
The ghetto was very well organized; it was like a little Jewish state. It even
had its own money with Rumkowski's picture on it; the money was called
"Rumkis." The ghetto stamps also bore his image.*

*Included in the ghetto administration were the Jewish police whose
main job was to keep order within the ghetto. Part of keeping order was to
send people to the notorious ghetto prison, a prison from which few people
returned. The Jewish police also presided at hangings for crimes committed in the ghetto. In addition, they helped to corral those selected for
deportation and to load them onto the death trains. They did much of the
Nazis' dirty work.*

*Although the responsibility of the Jewish police for keeping order and
administering justice within the ghetto was not to be envied, it was their
role in the round-ups, selections, and deportations that made them so
despised. During the Gehsperre, I had mostly positive impressions about
their actions. It seemed to me that by trying to restrain people, especially
the mothers and fathers, they probably lessened the violence and deaths
during those terrible days. Nevertheless, by controlling the people and by
shepherding the victims to the railroad station, the Jewish police made it
possible for the SS to complete their work with a minimum of manpower.
Nothing better illustrates how the Jewish police helped the Germans than
the final liquidation of the Lodz ghetto when only a few Germans were
involved in the deportation of some seventy thousand Jews. The story of the
Jewish police is indeed a dark and questionable one.*

*The first hanging that I witnessed involved a number of people who
were accused of sabotage in a leather factory. In order to teach us that the
punishment for sabotage would be severe, after work we were all forced
to march to the gallows to witness the executions. To emphasize the seri-
ousness of the crime, Biebow, Rumkowski, and many other high-ranking
officials were present. The executions were carried out by the Jewish police. I was quite far away from the gallows; nevertheless, I could hear the
condemned weeping and praying. It was the first time that I had witnessed
a hanging—one minute a person is alive and standing, and then he is hang-*

ing there lifeless. It was one of those moments, I will never forget. After the war, there were stories about sabotage in ghetto factories. Maybe it happened; if so, I never saw or heard about it.

Within the Nazi system of exploitation and control, my family and the other Jews of Lodz tried to maintain some semblance of normal life. As promised, my family was given an apartment in the building (Building Number 5, Wawelska Street) where my aunt Balcia Kantorowicz, her husband, and their seven daughters lived; it was on the third floor.[4] Our happiness at being reunited with our relatives was muted when we learned that two of our cousins had already been deported and that another was dying of tuberculosis. I would watch as she died—she was only thirteen.

Our apartment consisted of three rooms, and compared to our apartment in Pabianice it seemed small, cramped, dirty, and antiquated. However, we soon found out that it was luxurious compared to the lodgings of most people. My brother and I shared a bed in the kitchen, my sisters shared a bed in a small bedroom, and my parents slept in the living room. Sleeping was difficult, not because of the crowding, but because of the bugs. As soon as the lights were turned off, bugs would come out of the plaster walls; when you turned the lights back on, you could see them everywhere. Actually, we did not need to see the bugs to know that they were there; we could feel them as they crawled over our bodies and bit us. We always had bites, tiny red marks everywhere. Bugs were a plague throughout the ghetto.

Another thing that made sleeping difficult was that during the night we had to urinate several times because our diet consisted almost entirely of very watery soup. This circumstance, combined with the bugs, meant that sleeping through the night was a rarity. While getting up several times a night was annoying, it was excruciating in winter when the temperature fell below freezing. Neither we, nor anyone else in the ghetto, had heat. We barely had enough fuel to cook our meals, and there was none left to warm the rooms. I had a down comforter that kept me fairly warm while I was in the bed, but when I had to get up, there was nothing to protect me from the punishing Polish winter.

The worst part of our situation—worse than the cold and the bugs— was the lack of a toilet. As was true throughout the ghetto, our building lacked running water. This meant we had to carry our water from the well to the third floor—carrying water was one of my chores. It also meant that we had to share an outhouse in the backyard with everyone in the building. Since our family had had an indoor toilet in Pabianice, using a commu-

nal outhouse was a new and disgusting experience for me. The outhouse was almost always overflowing with sewage, and the smell was nauseating. When the water froze in the winter, the sewage backed up causing an already ghastly situation to become a nightmare. The stench and the sight of raw sewage made using the outhouse intolerable. I never became used to its sights or smells. I used it as little as possible. The outhouse at work was only minimally better. Sanitation throughout the ghetto was indeed primitive.

One good feature of our apartment was a balcony. Father used this little space to grow tomatoes and other vegetables like beets and lettuce to supplement our meager diet. People grew food wherever they could find space.

Cramped, bitten, and lacking heat and sanitation, we nevertheless had our family intact. Having a family to come home to, share concerns with, and embrace helped me cope with the hunger and fear which might otherwise have overwhelmed me. My family sustained me, and gave me a reason to live.

My parents' relationship, which had always been close, seemed to grow stronger as we faced ever greater adversity. They were kind to each other; I never heard them argue. They had to be worried about our situation and about the future, but they hid their fears from me as best they could. Occasionally, I overheard them talking about what was going to happen to us, but mostly they disguised their concerns. They tried to be positive and to shelter me from gloomy thoughts.

I especially remember how my parents comforted me whenever the SS appeared in the ghetto. The sight of the SS terrified me. You never knew what they would do— sometimes they snatched people and sometimes they seized property. I was a skinny little kid and the SS were big, or so they seemed to me. Their black uniforms were adorned with a death's head, and they carried guns and whips. Knowing how frightened I was, my parents would move close to me, and after the SS had left, they would comfort me with a hug and a kiss. I remember my mom saying to me, "Child, we will get through this." I was so frightened by the SS, that, even after I came to America, I was still afraid whenever I saw someone in uniform.

Our shared suffering strengthened my relationship with my sisters and my brother. I still remained closest to my sister Rozka, and I entrusted her with my fears and my hopes.

I also developed a very close relationship with my cousin Mala, the daughter of Aunt Balcia. Mala was very beautiful, and I liked her very

much. On the Sabbath, after I had finished carrying the water to our apartment and had completed my other chores, I would meet Mala and we would
walk, talk, and hold hands. You know, it has been years since I have even
thought of Mala; thinking of her now makes me sad. Our friendship meant
the world to me. It gave me a taste of what life could be like when we were
again free.

I remember our conversations. We would talk about life after the
ghetto, about going back to school, and about what we would become.
Interestingly, we always conceived of the future in terms of Poland, because that was where our families were. Strange as it may seem, I never
thought that the missing relatives were dead. I just assumed that they were
somewhere else and that they would return.

My sisters would tease me about Mala and say, "You can't marry your
first cousin because you will have stupid children." Well, the Germans
took care of that. The last time I saw Mala was when our family went into
hiding when the ghetto was being liquidated in 1944. I assume that she, her
parents, and her three sisters perished at Auschwitz-Birkenau. There were
no survivors in Mala's family.

But that was in the summer of 1944; in the meantime, we were all
working. In fact, the reason that the Lodz ghetto lasted as long as it did,
was that its factories were producing materials that were vital for the
German military. We produced everything imaginable. We had metal
factories where parts for trucks and cars were manufactured. We made
uniforms and boots for the soldiers and we produced pots, nails, furniture,
and many other necessary commodities. Everyone in Lodz worked. It was
not an option; if you didn't work, you didn't eat. Furthermore, as far as the
Germans were concerned, and as they had made abundantly clear during
the Gehsperre, if you could not work you were worthless.

Those of us who remained in the ghetto worked long hours, six days a
week. Saturday, the Jewish Sabbath, was the only day of rest. We were very
productive. The enormous output of our factories lulled us into believing
that the future of the ghetto was secure, that we would survive. We thought
that the Germans were rational, that they would want to keep the factories
humming and keep the workers producing. Why would they want to kill us
when we were doing such essential work?

Our family was fortunate in the jobs that we had. Father worked in a
place where clothes taken from the liquidated ghettos and from the victims
in the killing centers were brought to be sorted and repaired. The best of
the clothes were sent to Germany. The less good clothes were distributed in

the ghetto. It was an easy job for Father and it also meant that our family
received used but decent clothes. In fact, I believe that a coat Father found
for me may have saved my life during the selection at Auschwitz.

We also profited from the work of my sisters and my mother. Bluma
worked in a furniture factory making cribs and chairs. This helped us because sometimes she would be given wood shavings that were added to our
meager fuel ration. Rozka and Mother both worked in food kitchens, where
they were able to eat fairly good meals. This meant that the food ration for
our family could be stretched a little further. My brother worked in a large
metal factory that made ball bearings for cars and trucks. The experience
that he gained there served him well when he was sent to Auschwitz. There,
because of his skill, he was taken to a special dorm for metal-workers and
given three meals a day.

I worked in a factory where we made needles that were sent to
Germany and used for making rugs, carpets, sweaters, and other things.
All of the work had to be done by hand. Because it required a very gentle
touch, only teenagers were employed. Since I was good at the work, I soon
became an instructor for the new boys. I was also responsible for counting
the needles at the end of each day to make certain that we had reached the
quota set by the Germans. The work was boring and the hours long, so to
make the time go faster we would sing songs that were popular in the ghetto. You could hear the dinging of the hammer on the needles along with the
singing. It was a pretty sound and made our lives less dreary. Our favorite
song was about the young children who sold saccharine on the streets.

Our overseer was a German. He was a wonderful man, very sweet and
kind to us. He knew how hungry we were because a lot of the boys were so
weak that they could barely lift a hammer. He said that he tried to bring in
food but that the SS prohibited him from doing so. Sadly, a number of the
boys died of starvation or of diseases like tuberculosis and dysentery. I was
fortunate to be fairly healthy; I don't remember ever missing work.

One day that I will never forget, Rumkowski accompanied by some
high SS officials came to inspect our factory. Having the SS there was terrifying enough, but then Rumkowski singled me out to demonstrate how
we made the needles. I was scared to death; I was shaking. Petrified, I sat
down, and I did it. My reward was an affectionate pinch on the cheek, like
that of an uncle, showing his approval.

Our aunt, uncle, and cousins were also fortunate in that they all had
jobs. Mala worked in a factory where boots were made out of straw for the
soldiers to wear on the Eastern Front. First, the straw was braided, and

then it was sewn into large boots that were worn over the soldiers' shoes to provide warmth and also traction in the ice and snow.

From the German supervisors in Mala's factory and other factories, we picked up bits and pieces of information about the war which we scrutinized and dissected. From what we learned, it appeared that the Germans were having a tough time in Russia—we hoped this was true. The Germans who came to the factories never said that the army was retreating; rather, they said that it needed to relocate for strategic reasons.

Occasionally we heard news from sources in the Polish underground that confirmed our belief that the Soviet army was advancing. That was indeed glorious news. We also heard many rumors—some of which were actually true—but what we knew was at best random. For example, I knew about D-Day but not about Stalingrad, and, strangely, I knew about Tito and the partisans in Yugoslavia—what Hitler called his Fifth Front.

In a landscape with little humor, one play on words that circulated in the ghetto went like this:

"Who is going to be the loser of the war?"

*"The **Jid** or Yid [slang for Jew]: **J**apan, **I**taly and **D**eutschland (Germany)."*

Who is going to be the winner?"

*"The **Achse** [the Axis, German for an alliance of two or more powers]: the **A**mericans, **C**hinese, **S**oviets, and **E**urope."*

Although I did not know about it at the time, the one authentic source of news in the ghetto was a radio that one of the residents, an engineer named Widawski, constructed. Father listened to this radio; however, he did not tell me about it until after we were deported. Not only having a radio but also listening to one was punishable by death. Somehow, the Gestapo learned about the radio. When they came to arrest Widawski, he committed suicide so as not to betray anyone.

Once the radio was gone, we were cut off from any verifiable accounts of the war except our own eyes and ears. By the summer of 1944, we occasionally saw Allied planes flying eastward, and we could hear the artillery on the Eastern Front, presumably from the conflict raging in and around Warsaw. This could only be good news.

While momentous things were happening in the war, our regimented and routine life within the ghetto continued. Each working morning I got up, washed with a wash cloth, brushed my teeth, put on my clothes which, thanks to the efforts of my mom and my sisters were always clean and neat,

*and went to work. We were allowed a half-hour lunch break, during which
we received a bowl of watery potato soup and a small piece of bread.*

*After work I was too exhausted to do anything except trudge home,
eat more watery soup, and try to sleep. Saturday was the only day I had to
socialize. However, by the time I had completed all of my chores, there was
not a lot of day left. I tried to spend as much of the Sabbath as I could with
Mala—being with her gave me something to look forward to. Once, some
of us tried to play soccer, but there was really no place to play, and so we
quickly abandoned the effort. I did, however, fantasize about playing. I had
a hard time remembering that there was once a time when I had played
soccer and cowboys, gone to the movies, and read books. It must have been
another boy; it could not have been me.*

*The main amusement on the Sabbath for most people was to dress in
their best clothes and to walk around the ghetto. Our family, like many
ghetto dwellers, took a lot of pride in dressing nicely. We, of course, had an
advantage because of my father's work. Rozka as always looked stunning—
to me she was the most beautiful woman in the world. My father, who had
always been a fastidious dresser, continued to take pride in his appearance. On the Sabbath, he would dress with matching cuff links and tiepin.
Sometimes, when he had trouble locating a matching set, Mom would fuss
at him saying, "Do they have to match; don't you know there is a war going on?" Father, however, was insistent. Also, despite the difficulties that
it entailed, he was always clean shaven. I don't mean to be misleading,
we were among the fortunate few. Most people had little more than rags
to wear. However, when you see photographs of people walking along the
streets of the Lodz ghetto, many look quite presentable.*

*Worship was not a part of our Sabbath. There were no synagogues in
the ghetto, and although other people may have attended informal services
somewhere, our family did not. This did not mean that we abandoned our
faith; in fact, if anything, our faith deepened. As a family, we occasionally talked about God in relation to what was happening, but I don't ever
remember anyone blaming him or damning him for our situation. Mother,
as always, was the more religious parent, and Father, as before the war,
remained a staunch Zionist—his religious beliefs were inseparable from his
Zionism.*

*Even though we did not attend services, we did keep the Jewish tradi-
tions. Despite having very little food to put on the table, we did celebrate
the Sabbath meal with our best table cloth and dishes, and we lit candles.
We observed Passover, Rosh Hashanah, and Yom Kippur. I vaguely remem-*

ber that there were special rooms that we used for the high holy days, but I can't be precise about that. I do not remember celebrating Hanukkah. With its candies and gifts, celebrating Hanukkah was not appropriate, much less feasible, in the Lodz ghetto.

It was difficult to keep up with time. Whereas before the war, life seemed to move from one special day to the next, life in the ghetto seemed to lurch forward in some strange way without reference to the calendar. We lost any concept of time except in relation to how many days there were until we would get rations. We all knew when the food was coming; it was the only unit of time that mattered. Food was the main topic of conversation.

One of the supervisors in my factory, an engineer from Vienna named Fisher, was obsessed by food. He talked constantly about how many kilograms of this or that we would receive—he could talk of nothing else. His constant jabbering about food and rations was annoying. Try hard as I might to silence my hunger and to think about other things, Fisher would make it a priority. He was not alone in his obsession.

We usually received our rations every ten days, and, as anxious as we were for food, the process of obtaining it was grueling. First, we had to stand in a line to receive the ration card. Each family received one card with the rations for the entire family. You then had to stand in another line to receive the food allotment, and after that, you had to stand in a third line to receive the bread allotment. I hated standing in those lines. I would be exhausted from work, and then I would have to stand and wait and wait in some line. Our family took turns, and that made it a little more bearable.

The rations that we received were small, and the quality of the food was poor. We had barely enough food to survive for a few days, much less ten. The bread was not really bread; I don't know what it was made of, but it was rumored to contain a lot of sawdust. We received enough for each of us to have a small slice of bread each day. The food ration consisted mainly of potatoes, unbleached flour, and kohlrabi, a vegetable, similar to a broccoli stem or a cabbage core. Kohlrabi was disgusting; I absolutely hated it. Occasionally we received beets, radishes, cabbage, or turnips, and sometimes we got a can of horse meat, some margarine, or a little brown sugar. On rare occasions, we would receive potato peels—yes, potato peels. They were extra food, and were considered a reason to celebrate.

Our diet consisted almost entirely of soup—watery soup with potatoes and maybe a vegetable or two. This watery diet caused our stomachs to swell, and made us need to urinate often. We had almost no protein. The rations were so minimal that we would have had difficulty surviving had not Mother and Rachael worked in places that served food. Like everyone else in the ghetto, we were always hungry.

The hunger that we endured is impossible to describe. It was always there; it never disappeared. I dreamt of food; I fantasized about chocolate and salami and herring— but mostly I just wanted bread, all of the bread that I could possibly eat. A lot of people lost their minds from hunger. The hunger was so great that there were many cases of families who hid the bodies of their deceased for weeks rather than reporting the death, because the family wanted to continue to receive the rations allotted to that person. Perhaps the saddest cases were those people who gobbled their rations in the first few days and then starved to death before the next distribution. This is one of the reasons that the death rate was so high. In our family, we were very careful to make our rations last. It was not an easy task.

Yes, the hunger was so terrible that there were times when I really didn't care to go on any longer, but fear of dying was greater than the hunger. It didn't help to sit and bemoan the circumstances; so I tried to accept the situation, adjust, and make the best of it. That was not always easy to do, but I was born with an optimistic and cheerful outlook. These innate qualities helped me to plod on.

Another way in which the Jews in the ghetto suffered was from the cold. Polish winters are ruthless, and when you are very thin and have virtually no heat, they are unbearable. Death by freezing was not uncommon. I heard stories of ghetto residents tearing down buildings to get wood and then fighting over the boards. I do not know of any homes that had heat; the factories were a little better. The one where I worked had to be kept warm enough so that the machinery would not be harmed. However, I am certain that the heat never rose above the minimum required to keep the machines running safely. But then that was all that mattered. Machines were expensive; workers were expendable.

Added to the hunger and cold was the constant sight of the dead and dying. Everywhere there were beggars—skeletons crying for food. There was nothing to do but to ignore them. We were surrounded by the bodies of dead people. When I went to work there would be corpses on the streets; this was especially true during the winter. After a while, I became almost inured to the sight of dead people. In addition, there were the carts filled with corpses, maybe twenty to thirty bodies in a cart. These carts were pulled by skeletal men, women, and children who were just one step away from death themselves. People were dying in such large numbers that the ghetto was forced to resort to mass, unmarked graves where the bodies were just dumped in one after another.

It really bothered me that there was no commemoration of the dead in the ghetto. A family member would die, and the next day you went to work. It was as though people became robots without hearts and without tears. Actually, they lacked the time, energy, or means to pay their respects in any conventional way. Just take the dead, put them in a cart, and keep going. I never became used to this.

One thing that gave me a little extra edge against hunger was that I was chosen to attend some special dinners that Rumkowski held for teens. Rumkowski was known to have a special regard for children—he had worked in an orphanage before the war. Since there were no young children left in the ghetto after the Gehsperre, he turned his attention to the teens and began to sponsor special dinners for some who worked in the factories. I was given a coupon to attend because of my job in the needle factory. On the evenings of the dinners, I would dress in my best clothes and go to a special kitchen. There we sat at long tables and received a beautiful dinner of bread with margarine, horse meat, potatoes, and vegetables. I would attend for two weeks, and then I would stop for two weeks and then start again. This two-week cycle was repeated for a number of months—I'm not certain how many. It was wonderful while it lasted. The food was great, and the dinners gave me a chance to meet and socialize with other people my age and to forget the dreariness of my life for a little while.

In an effort to raise the spirits of all the young people, the ghetto administration sponsored what was called the Ghetto Review, a show in which talented teens performed.[5] Since our instruments had been confiscated and no one had the energy to dance, the talent consisted almost exclusively of singing and skits. The songs were mostly sad songs about ghetto life, and the main subject was hunger, food, and rations.[6] I remember one especially sad song about the cemetery and another about dreams for a life beyond the ghetto. For some reason, I remember a performance by a boy and girl in which the girl bragged that she will make the boy laugh. He replied, "How can I possibly laugh when I have not eaten in weeks and my mother is dying?" She responded, "I will give you a roll with butter and herring!" "Yes," he shouted, "that will make me laugh."

Singing was one of the few amusements that remained for us, and songs became a part of our collective identity. I have already mentioned how we sang at work and how the voices and the dinging of the hammers blended together. I believe that everyone who survived the ghetto *could sing some of the ghetto songs. The one song that we all knew was "Rumkowski Chaim." I can still remember the refrain. This song described how, as when the Jews were in the desert they were fed manna from heaven, now Rumkowski will feed the Jews in the ghetto.[7] Another song that I remember described the cries of children who illegally sold saccharine on the street. I remember seeing these children and hearing their pitiful pleas.*

Other than the Saturday walks with Mala, Rumkowski's dinners, and an occasional talent show, there was little to break the monotony of my life in the ghetto. I still attended Zionist meetings, but they did not excite and motivate me as they had in Pabianice. Mainly, this was because I was simply too hungry, cold, and tired by the end of the day to care much about Zionism or anything else. I attended the meetings more to see my friends than out of any convictions. In particular, I enjoyed seeing Gershon, my friend from Pabianice. Poor Gershon, not long after he came to the ghetto, his father died and his mother was deported in the Gehsperre. Later, he developed a problem with his knees and was unable to walk or to work. Gershon undoubtedly would not have survived had not our Zionist group raised money to buy some medicine that restored the use of his legs. This saved his life.

Speaking of Gershon reminds me of Abraham, my best childhood friend. The last time I saw Abraham was in May 1942, before the Pabianice ghetto was liquidated. As best I can piece together, Abraham was in the group that was sent to Lodz. From Lodz he was sent to Dombrovo, a neighboring town, where he worked cleaning the local ghettos which had been liquidated. It was work much like I had done in Pabianice. It appears that Abraham became sick and died there. I did not know about his death until after the war, when I learned about it from a friend of my brother's who was in Dombrovo with him.

After a year and a half without deportations, by the spring of 1944 we were beginning to think that maybe, just maybe, we would survive, that we would outlive the war. We were turning out an enormous amount of items essential to the German military, and we felt assured that this productivity insulated us against death. We simply could not imagine that a people as logical as the Germans would bite the hand that was feeding them. Yes, the Germans were logical, but unfortunately for us, they followed their logic even when it was self-destructive. At the heart of Nazism was the goal of creating a Master Race, primarily by eliminating inferior races and people. In the final year of the war, attaining this goal took precedence over winning the war. The Lodz Jews would perish.

The liquidation of the ghetto was announced in the late spring of 1944, and the death trains began departing for Chelmno and Auschwitz in late June. They continued almost nonstop until August. Our family must have been on one of the last trains to leave.

Even before the trains began to roll, the SS mounted an energetic campaign to convince us that it was in our best interests to leave. They announced over and over that for strategic reasons (they never said the Germans were retreating), they needed to evacuate Lodz and relocate the factories in Germany, where we would resume our work. They enticed us by talking about the bakeries in Germany and the abundance of food. I remember that Biebow, the SS officer in charge of the ghetto, came into the yard of the building where we lived and talked to us about the need to liquidate the ghetto. In a very kind and pleasing voice, he said, "We have bakeries in Germany and we will feed you with very fine bread, and you will continue to work, and you will be clean and well." Sometimes the leaders of the ghetto, Rumkowski among them, stood with the SS and urged us to leave voluntarily.

All of this deception was to prevent any kind of panic and any resistance. The Nazis wanted to lure us into the trains, so that they would only need a small crew to oversee the deportation of tens of thousands of Jews. Above all, the Germans did not want any trouble. Although I did not know it then, I now know that they had experienced massive resistance when liquidating the Warsaw ghetto, and they did not want a similar scenario in Lodz. So they doubled their efforts to deceive us.

About a week after the evacuation announcement when it became obvious that few Jews would volunteer for the transports, the Germans began to force us into the trains. They would seal off an area and then march the captured Jews to the station. At this point, my family went into hiding.

Our hiding place was in the basement of a former soup kitchen. The manager of the kitchen was a friend of my parents, and my mother had worked there. Hiding there with our family were the manager, his wife, and his two children, and the manager's brother, his wife, and his three children. There were fifteen people in all. Fortunately, our hiding place was fairly large—we could all sit at the same time—and it was not too primitive. While I was totally ignorant about the plan to hide, it was obvious that preparations had been made well in advance. Canned goods, flour, potatoes, and even aspirin and Band-Aids had been stored there. We thought we could manage because we were sure that the Soviet army would liberate us shortly.

I don't remember how long we stayed in the cellar, but it must have been a number of weeks. After the first week or so, we began to leave the cellar at night to get some fresh air, and sometimes we slept on the floor of the kitchen. It was quiet at night because there were no roundups or transports—the Germans were wary of being in the ghetto after dark. During the day, we stayed in the cellar and wrote in journals, played checkers or cards, and read; we did not talk much because there was so little oxygen. After we had been in hiding about two weeks, we started to hear the Germans announcing on loudspeakers that anyone found hiding in basements, attics, or anywhere else would be shot on the spot. It was not long before we heard shots signaling executions.

The announcement and the shots caused some of us, especially the younger ones like me, to wonder whether hiding was the best plan. We started saying things such as, "Look, if the Germans find us, they will shoot us immediately, but, if we go to Germany to work, we will have a chance to survive." The more shots that we heard, the more afraid we became of being discovered, and the more convinced some of us became, including me, that we should leave our hiding place and join the deportees. Finally, my father said, "Let's make a decision, and let's do it democratically by a vote using a secret ballot. Whatever the majority decides is what we will do." Later, Father said things to me that suggested that he was fairly sure of the fate that awaited us once we were on the trains. Nevertheless, he was not certain, and so he did not try to persuade us. The majority voted to come forward. Most of the young people felt relief and were happy; most of the adults were not happy.

Once the decision was made, we dressed in our best clothes and started walking toward the train station. We were soon joined by an escort of Jewish police who helped us walk up a plank into a cattle car. Once we were in the cattle car and the door was sealed, we knew we had made a mistake. Unfortunately, it was too late. We were now headed for Auschwitz, a place I had never heard of.

1. Sierakowiak, *(Lodz) Diary*. Dawid's diary begins on June 28, 1939. It ends in the summer of 1943, several months before he died, probably from tuberculosis. Throughout his diary, Dawid talks about "connections" and how they protected the people who had them. He assails the two-class system, those with "connections" and those without, that existed in the ghetto. In his entry for April 5, 1943 (266-267), he states,

Those in the ruling class in the ghetto are provided with everything in abundance. The division between classes in the ghetto has become complete. In hardly any respect can you compare the fate of a supervisor with the fate of a worker. The workers are dying at a terrifying rate, while the ruling class lives in growing prosperity. The only way to survive the war is to join the higher classes.

Sierakowiak lived in Building Number 9 on Wawelska Street. Morris lived on the same street but did not know him.

2. In his speech to the ghetto, announcing that the Germans had demanded a large number of deportees, Rumkowski stated,

"The ghetto has been struck a hard blow. They demand what is most dear to it—children and old people ...I never imagined that my own hands would be forced to make this sacrifice on the altar. In my old age I am forced to stretch out my hands and to beg: "Brothers and sisters, give them to me!—Fathers and mothers, give me your children."

Chaim Rumkowski, "Rumkowski's Address at the Time of the Deportation of the Children from the Lodz Ghetto, September 4, 1942," in Botwinick, *A Holocaust Reader*, 150.

3. Hans Biebow was tried and executed in Poland in the spring of 1947.

4. "My mother also had a brother Ichio [Issac] who had lived in Lodz. He and his wife and two children left before we arrived. They may have gone to Warsaw where his wife's family lived. I do not know what happened to them but since we never saw or heard of them again, I presume that they did not survive." Morris Glass

5. The ghetto leaders tried to make life as pleasant as possible by sponsoring cultural events like concerts, plays, readings, and art exhibits.

6. Flam, *Singing for Survival*, 102. "The theme of hunger dominates all the street songs [discussed in the chapter]. Four songs out of the eighteen speak directly about hunger, and five others describe food. Two refer to the subject of hunger by talking about the theft of food or food coupons."

7. Flam, *Singing for Survival*, 37-47. Included in these pages are all the verses and the refrain to the song, "Rumkowshi Chaim," and also some interesting variants. Flam calls this song, "the ghetto's greatest 'hit'" (37), and she corroborates Morris's assertion that everyone knew this song, "The song, especially the refrain, is known to every survivor of the Lodz ghetto" (42). The first lines of the refrain, included on page 90, are:

Because [he is] our Chaim
He gives us bran,
He gives us barley,
He gives us manna.

Chapter 9

Deportation and Auschwitz

The Deportation System

The slamming of the door to the cattle car signaled the end of one phase of my life in the Holocaust and the beginning of a new one. Nothing that I had experienced before had or could have prepared me for the absolute hell that I now entered. It was a landscape composed of primitive camps, starvation, violence, selections, and death on an unimaginable scale. It was for me a time of loss. I lost my mother, my sisters, and my father in the Nazi camps. Somehow, I managed to survive. Morris Glass

If science and technology shaped the form of the murder, the machine that linked the various parts of the Nazi killing industry was the train. Almost all transportation to the killing centers was by rail. Generally about a hundred people were crammed into cattle cars with only a pail for excrement, virtually no ventilation, and little or no food or water. Those who have related their experiences tell of the horror of the trip—the heat, thirst, filth, dark, and fear. Even a short trip often took several days as trains were often idled to accommodate the competing needs of the army or the Ministry of War Production. When the distance was long, a trip might take over a week. Many died in transit. Some went mad; virtually all were traumatized by the experience.[1]

The organization and administration of the death trains was a daunting task. Trains had to be requisitioned, time on the tracks arranged, and schedules for departures and arrivals drawn up. Additionally, arrangements had to be made for assembling the victims at the stations and for receiving them at the death camps. The Germans also had to pay the railroad companies—the usual charge was third-class fare for adults, half-price for children under ten, and no charge for those under four. If there were over four hundred passengers, then a group fare that was half the third-class rate was applied. This was of course the charge for a one-way trip; round-trip tickets were only needed for the guards.[2]

It is estimated that more than 3,000,000 Jews, Gypsies, and other "undesirables" were transported by trains to the killing centers. While the death trains carried victims from all the countries of occupied Europe, Polish Jews constituted by far the largest group, approximately 2,200,000 persons. Undoubtedly, one of the most intense periods of deportation occurred in the late summer and early fall of 1942. During this time, approximately 300,000 Jews from Warsaw were shipped to Treblinka, a killing center located 65 miles northeast of the city. At Treblinka, it is estimated that 874,000 persons were murdered in a little over a year.

In 1942, the Jews in the Warsaw ghetto assembled and entered the trains fairly submissively. However, when the deportations resumed in 1943, the response was quite different. Knowing full well their destination and fate, the 70,000 Jews remaining in Warsaw resisted. The resulting Warsaw Ghetto Uprising, which lasted from April 19 through mid-May, was doomed from the beginning—virtually all of the Jews were killed or deported, and the ghetto was leveled. Nevertheless, this uprising stands as a symbol of Jewish courage in the face of overwhelming odds. It is also seen as the turning point in the two-thousand-year history of Jewish passivity and submission to oppression. Unfortunately, the sustained resistance in Warsaw stands as a unique event; elsewhere, with only a few exceptions, the Jews assembled at the stations and entered the trains reluctantly but compliantly.

The resistance in Warsaw was the nightmare that the Nazis had long feared and tried to prevent. Docility was the response that they desired and they worked diligently to achieve it. Their main strategy was to lure their victims by promises. They promised the Jews that they would be resettled farther east and added that the first to go would have access to the best lands, that families would be kept together, and that no harm would come to anyone. To the starving ghetto Jews, the Germans promised bread to those who would voluntarily report for deportation. The Germans also lulled their victims by telling them what tools they needed to bring for use in their new life and the precise amount of luggage that they could take.

Even as late as August 1944, when Morris's group decided to abandon their hiding place and report for deportation, he notes that at least some were duped by the idea that they would be resettled in Germany, where workers were needed and conditions were better. The Germans must be credited with a successful campaign of deception. In this they were helped by their victims' longing to believe that what they were hearing was indeed true.

My Journey from Lodz to Auschwitz

Even though the distance between Lodz and Auschwitz was only a few hundred miles, our trip in the cattle car took several days. They were terrible, terrible days—an appropriate prelude to the horror that was to follow. Often, our train was stopped for extended periods to let other trains pass. As I peeked through the cracks, I could see that these trains were full of soldiers. Thus, what should have been a relatively short trip became a very long one.

There were only about eighty people in our car; this meant that at least we could sit to sleep. There was no sanitation except a bucket in a corner. Some of the men vainly tried to hang clothes around it in order to provide a minimum of privacy. It was August and it was hot. There was no ventilation, and the smell of excrement and sweating bodies was awful. Some people died. The dead were thrown out when the doors were occasionally opened so that the guards could give us a little water and bread. During most of the journey, the car was quiet; we hardly spoke to each other. Some prayed. I remember people being kind to one another.

I passed most of the time looking through the cracks and wondering where we were going and what would happen to us. When we left Lodz I had thought—maybe I should say that I had persuaded myself to believe— that we were going to Germany. However, it soon became apparent that we were not headed west toward Germany, but that we were in fact headed southeast. This, I knew, was not good. Wherever we were going, I prayed that my family and I would be spared the worst. I hoped that we might be taken to a work camp, but because of the way we were being treated, I knew deep down that this was not the case. Now I began to fear that the rumors of murder, which I had dismissed as nonsense, might indeed be true. The fear and the dread were paralyzing.

My only comfort during this terrifying journey was that my family was together in the same car. Being with my family had sustained me through my four and a half years in the ghettoes, and it sustained me during this horrible journey. We held hands and when I cried my mom would say, "My child, we will be together; we will be together." However, when the train finally stopped and the doors of the cattle car were opened, my fears became reality. I knew we had arrived in hell.

Auschwitz and the Camp System
(Auschwitz is the German name for the Polish town of Oswiecim.)

"Hell" was Auschwitz—the place that more than any other has come to symbolize the Holocaust—and rightly so. It is estimated that at least 1,200,000 people, about 90 percent of whom were Jews, were murdered there.[3] Located in southern Poland near the border with Czechoslovakia, Auschwitz was situated at the center of a web of railroad lines coming from all over Europe. This made it the perfect spot for the Nazis to establish a killing center. It was at Auschwitz that the greatest number of victims was murdered. It was there that thousands were worked to death, and it was there that many others were processed before being shipped to various concentration camps in Germany, Poland, and elsewhere. Auschwitz was an enormous place with a variety of functions.

The name "Auschwitz" is associated with three separate camps that were connected by location and function: Auschwitz I; Birkenau or Auschwitz II; and Monowitz or Auschwitz III. Auschwitz I was the original camp; the others were built later. Auschwitz I housed administrative offices, dormitories for the SS and their auxiliaries, and barracks for some prisoners. It also included workshops and one crematorium (the term crematorium includes both the gas chambers and the ovens for cremating the bodies). Auschwitz I is the section of the complex that is most intact today. Its entrance bears the famous sign, "Arbeit Macht Frei" [Work Makes Free].

Birkenau, or Auschwitz II, was located about two miles from Auschwitz I. Built expressly as a killing center, Birkenau housed the four crematoria where most of the murders occurred. It was through the opening of the entrance tower to Birkenau that the death trains passed on their way to a ramp where the victims disembarked and the SS selected those who would immediately die and those who would work as slaves for the Third Reich.

Birkenau was a huge camp. In addition to the crematoria, it included many, many barracks housing thousands of inmates who worked there or in nearby factories. It also served as a transit camp for prisoners who were subsequently sent to other camps—Morris belonged to this group. Birkenau was also the place where Mengele and other SS doctors conducted their infamous medical experiments.

Because the Germans destroyed most of the wooden barracks and much of the crematoria before they retreated, there is little remaining at Birkenau today. The remains of the crematoria are rapidly decaying due to the swampy conditions in the area. A heated discussion is presently taking place as to whether to restore the crematoria or to let them continue to deteriorate. A decision has not yet been made.

The third camp, Monowitz or Auschwitz III, was the site of Buna, a huge rubber factory run by I. G. Farben. In addition to Buna, the Auschwitz complex included some forty smaller satellite camps where slave laborers worked for the Germans.

As the preceding suggests, Auschwitz served the Nazis in a variety of ways. It is because it functioned as a concentration camp and a transit camp as well as a killing center that there were survivors of Auschwitz. If it had been only a killing center, there would have been few if any survivors. There were almost no survivors of Birkenau or of the other places that were built solely to murder people.

The variety of functions that took place at Auschwitz made it unique in the Nazi camp system. Generally the Nazis designated different camps to perform specific tasks, and the various camps can be categorized on the basis of their primary function: detention/work camps, death camps, and transit camps. It should be noted that occasionally the functions overlapped, as illustrated by Auschwitz. Sometimes the functions changed, as illustrated by the shift of the detention camps to work camps during the war. Whatever their purpose, all of the camps ultimately became involved in the destruction of the Jews.

The Nazis established concentration camps as soon as they came to power in 1933. These camps functioned as places to hold and re-educate their political opponents, mainly Socialists, Communists, and liberals. The first, Dachau, was built near Munich, Germany, in 1933. Other concentration camps whose names may be familiar were Buchenwald, Bergen-Belsen, Ravensbruck, Mauthausen, and, of course, Auschwitz. Over time, the number of these camps increased— during the war years, they increased exponentially. The Nazis also expanded the categories of people that they imprisoned to include "asocial" elements like homosexuals, Jehovah's Witnesses, criminals and, after Kristallnacht in 1938, the Jews.

Before World War II began, even though the camps were brutal, being imprisoned in one was not necessarily a death sentence. In fact, it was possible for the inmates, including Jews, to be released. The function of the detention camps changed during the war when the need for labor transformed most of them into slave labor camps—places where the inmates were literally worked to death. By the end of the war, there were hundreds and hundreds of such camps. Nevertheless, despite horrific conditions within them, it was possible to survive such a place.

In contrast to the concentration/work camps, the death camps existed only to kill, and there were almost no survivors of these places. The victims were primarily, but not exclusively, Jews. There were six killing centers—Birkenau-Auschwitz, Treblinka, Belzec, Majdanek, Sobibor, and Chelmno. All were located in Poland on sites that were close to large Jewish populations and that had access to railroad lines. Five of the killing centers functioned primarily to murder Polish Jews. Birkenau, however, with train lines from much of Europe converging there, functioned as an international death camp where victims from southern, central, and western Europe were sent. Because of this, the room at Birkenau where the victims undressed before entering the gas chambers was called the "International Information Center." Signs in many languages were posted there.

The death camps were small; in fact, considering the number of people killed in them, they were amazingly small. These places did not need to be large since the victims were gassed and their bodies disposed of within hours after their arrival. For example, Chelmno, the first killing center to be operational and the one closest to Lodz, consisted of one building (first a castle and later a church) where the victims undressed. They were then loaded into vans, where they were gassed; their bodies were dumped into pits in a nearby forest.

Since the Nazis wanted to "process" the "pieces" as quickly and as smoothly as possible, the killing centers were designed to be both efficient and deceptive. To this end the Nazis strove to give their victims the illusion that nothing bad was going to happen to them. The deception was maintained until the moment that they entered the gas chambers. At Treblinka the arrival platform was disguised as a pretty little country station with curtains painted in fake windows, bogus time tables and fake ticket counters, and real flowers. At some camps, an orchestra welcomed the trains. At Birkenau, the victims were instructed to remember the number of the hook on which they had hung their clothes so that they could reclaim them later. Almost always there were promises that after the "baths," the victims would be assigned work. For the most part, the deception worked. If everything went as planned, and usually it did, the entire process took only a few hours.

In all of the death camps, the agent of death was gas, the use of which had been perfected in the process of euthanizing some fifty thousand or more physically and mentally handicapped German citizens. At Chelmno, the victims were asphyxiated with carbon monoxide in vans designed expressly for that purpose. Three camps, Treblinka, Sobibor, and Belzec, used carbon monoxide produced by stationary engines. At Birkenau and Majdanek, a pesticide, Zyklon B, was used.

While they differed slightly in the method of killing their victims, all of the camps relied on prisoners to do various jobs. Although the SS were in charge of the camps and held the key administrative positions, their actual numbers were small. To augment the work force, the SS used auxiliaries from Ukraine, Latvia, and elsewhere, but mainly they relied on the prisoners. For the highest positions, the SS preferred German prisoners, either criminals or political prisoners, but other prisoners, including Jews, held posts with some authority. The Jews were mainly used for the most lowly and nasty tasks like emptying and cleaning the trains and the gas chambers, cutting hair and pulling teeth, burying the bodies, and later exhuming and burning them. The Jews who did this work were part of what was called the *Sonderkommando* [special work units]. These were the people who "greeted" Morris on his arrival at Auschwitz.

The third category of camps was the transit or internment camp. These were places where the Nazis corralled their victims until they were deported to either a death or work camp. The most famous of these camps were Drancy, near Paris; Westerbork in the Netherlands (Anne Frank was taken there); and Theresienstadt in Czechoslovakia. Although the situation of the inmates varied from camp to camp, generally their stay was short. Auschwitz functioned as a transit camp for Morris. In August 1944, he was shipped from Lodz to Auschwitz, where he stayed for about six weeks before he was sent to the Dachau camps.

My Weeks at Auschwitz
(mid-August through September 1944)

We arrived at Birkenau, I would say, at about eleven in the morning on a beautiful summer day. As soon as the door of the cattle car was opened, I knew that I was in a terrible place. The first thing that I noticed was the smell—the horrible stench of burning bodies. It was a smell that I could not then identify but that I came to know well during the following weeks. Next, I saw chimneys belching smoke—I didn't immediately connect the smell and the smoke. I noticed the wire fences which, in contrast to Lodz, were smooth, not barbed; I knew this meant that they were electrical and deadly. I saw the watchtowers, the SS with their dogs, and a lot of men dressed in striped clothing. These, I later learned, were Jewish prisoners who were part of the Sonderkommando.

The scene as we descended from the cars was chaotic and terrifying. While shouting, "Hurry, hurry, hurry," the Jewish prisoners pushed the men to one side and the women, children, and elderly to the other. Once we were separated, they marched us a short distance to the place where the selections were being made. While we were walking, the Sonderkommandos kept telling us to be quiet and to try to look our best.

Standing in a line behind my father and my brother, I kept moving until I was in front of the infamous Dr. Mengele, the "Angel of Death,"—at least I'm fairly certain that it was he. Although I was ignorant as to what was happening, I did know that I desperately wanted to stay with my father and brother. When it was my turn to stand in front of Mengele, he hesitated. While I did not understand it then, I now know that he was playing God—he was deciding whether I was big and healthy enough to work for the Third Reich or whether I should die immediately. He looked me over and finally motioned for me to go the same way as my father and brother. I was so happy. I have always believed that what saved me was the coat that I was wearing—a plaid coat with enormous shoulder pads. This coat made me, a skinny, little kid who was not very developed, look a lot larger than I was. That was something that I thought about later; at the time, my only thought was relief that I had been sent in the same direction as my father and brother.

After the selection, we were taken to be processed. As I marched away, I glimpsed my mother and two sisters for the last time. I waved to them, and they waved back. I never saw them again. Although they survived the selection and Auschwitz, they did not survive the Holocaust. That last glimpse is engraved in my mind and has remained with me through the years. I still have nightmares in which I relive that final moment. The nightmares are not as frequent as they once were, but they still return. I believe that I will always be haunted by that scene. I wish to God that he would give me just one moment so that I could tell my mom how much I loved her, and my sisters how much I loved them—just one moment.[4]

From the selection area, we were marched to a huge complex known as the Sauna where we were processed.⁵ I had no knowledge of what would happen to us there; I had only fears. First, we were taken into a room and told to undress. Everything was taken from us except for our shoes and our belts. These were ripped open to make sure that no valuables were hidden in them. Unfortunately, my brother was wearing a fairly nice pair of shoes. These were snatched from him and replaced with some wooden ones. Shoes were critical to survival in the camps, and since wooden shoes cut the flesh, they were virtually a death sentence. Luckily for my brother, a friend was able to procure some leather shoes for him. Otherwise, I don't believe that he would have survived.

After undressing we were sent to another big room where all of our body hair was shaved off. Then they brushed a disinfectant on us. It burnt. My skin felt like it was on fire. After the disinfectant, we went through a door into the showers to wash. I did not know, at the time, that elsewhere in the camp the nozzles spewed gas and not water.

While we were standing naked in the shower room, the SS swooped in for a second selection. They began to look us over and to cull those who may have appeared able- bodied when dressed but whose nakedness re-vealed hernias and other imperfections. I had reason to be fearful because without my plaid coat, I looked like the skinny, little kid that I was. Some of the men, realizing that I was vulnerable, yelled to me to stretch out on the floor next to a long wooden bench. Then with their legs and feet, they hid me from the eyes of the SS. A lot of men were taken away to be gassed, but thanks to the quick thinking of those men, I survived this second selection.

After we had showered, we were driven into another room and given our prison uniforms—striped pants, a jacket, and a hat. There was no ef-fort to match the size of the person with the clothes. Then we went outside. Once outside, I began frantically looking for my father. I searched and searched through a sea of faces, but I could not find him. Suddenly, I real-ized that the person standing next to me was my father! My own father—he was standing next to me, and I had not recognized him! The experience of the last few hours had transformed him. His face was haggard and grey and he seemed to have aged thirty years in just a few hours. I now know that he knew exactly where we were; that he knew the horrible smell was burning flesh, and that he knew he would never again see his wife and daughters. I was aware that our situation was bad, but I did not realize how grim it actually was. Father did!

While being processed, we were not tattooed with a number. I re-

*ceived my number later at one of the Dachau camps and not while I was
at Auschwitz—my number was definitely not an Auschwitz number. As far
as I know we were never even registered at Auschwitz. Evidently from the
beginning, my father, my brother, and I were designated to be shipped out
of Auschwitz to work somewhere else, and thus registration and tattooing
were irrelevant.*

*After standing outside the Sauna for quite awhile, we were marched to
that part of the camp where the prisoners were housed. Here were numerous wooden barracks, rows and rows and rows of them. The barracks were
grouped into what were called camps, each of which was made up of about
thirty barracks surrounded by wire. Each camp was designated by a letter. Some of camps also acquired special names because of the particular
groups housed there. We were taken to Camp E, known as the Gypsy Camp.
I learned later that the Gypsies had been sent to the gas chambers in order
to make room for us.[6]*

*When we arrived at the Gypsy Camp, we were assigned to barracks
with what seemed to be hundreds of other men. Here, we were met by the
barracks leaders, called Kapos. The Kapos gave us a welcome that was
not pretty. "You are in Auschwitz," they said, "and here you must obey
orders to the fullest. If you don't, you will go to the frying pan." Following
this ominous orientation, we were given soup and allowed to sleep sitting
scrunched together on a concrete slab—there was no room to lie down.
After a harrowing day that had left my mind full of questions and my soul
in agony, sleep did not come easily. In fact, I do not remember sleeping at
all.*

*A few days after arriving at the Gypsy Camp, we were able to trans-
fer from our original barracks to one where Nonek, my friend Abraham's
brother and my sister Bluma's boyfriend, was a Kapo. Since he was a
Kapo, Nonek had a small enclosure to himself off the main room and a bed.
It was Nonek who found the shoes for my brother that saved his life; before
I left Auschwitz, Nonek would also save mine.[7]*

*Although during my first day at Auschwitz I had not really understood
our situation, it was not long before I became fully aware of where I was
and of the atrocities that were being committed there. It was impossible
to deny the horror of the place. Our camp was located near Crematoria
III. Day and night we could see the chimneys spouting fire and smoke and
smell the horrible stench that came from them. After several days, I finally
acknowledged that the smoke and the overpowering smell were related,
and that they were the product of burning human bodies. The odor of burn-*

ing flesh is very distinct. Once you have smelled it, the smell is impossible to forget. The smell must have drifted over a large area, and the smoke and flames must have been visible for miles. I say all of this because the people who lived in the area and who say that they didn't know what was going on—well, how could they not have known!

I also came to realize that there was no chance of escape. Electric fences were everywhere, and towers with machine guns manned by the SS or their auxiliaries were stationed along them. Even escape by suicide was denied since we were not allowed near the fences. At Auschwitz, the Germans controlled everything. They were, as they themselves said, "Lords of the World." The Germans even controlled the time and manner of their victims' deaths. This was intentional. At the time, I was too young to understand the totality of the control that they exerted over us.

At Auschwitz, and also in the other camps where I was imprisoned, we were totally isolated from the rest of the world. We had no knowledge of anything beyond the confines of our camp. We had no calendars, no watches—there was no way to calculate time except by the seasons and the Christian holidays. Traditional measurements of time became meaningless. Days went by—that was about all we knew. We stopped being humans. We were just bodies trying to stay warm, to get more soup, to do whatever we could to stay alive a little while longer.

Life at Birkenau followed a daily routine. Very early in the morning, just about daylight, a siren woke us up. Immediately, we went outside for roll call, or as it was known, "Appell." The whole camp had to form lines of five and stand at attention while the Kapos counted and recounted the prisoners to make certain that everyone was present. This always took an hour or more; sometimes it took several hours. Even though it was summer, the mornings were often very cold. To keep warm, we would huddle as close as possible, forming what we called a human furnace. Later, when I was in the Dachau camps during the winter, this tactic was crucial to surviving.

Since removing one's hat was mandatory when encountering a German, during the first roll call we were taught "hats on, hats off." Subsequently, we were forced to practice this exercise endlessly, for no other reason than to remind us of the power that the Nazis had over us. When we did not line up quickly enough, or the count was wrong, or we moved, or did anything that displeased them, the Kapos would punch or hit us with their sticks. In sum, the roll calls were mindless, tiring, and often violent. Like so much else, roll call was just one more way to make our lives miserable.

After roll call, we had little to do. Occasionally, we had an opportunity to help the local farmers. This offered the possibility of obtaining extra food; so we jumped at the chance. Mostly, we did nothing. We didn't socialize or talk much. I don't know why; that is just the way it was. When the weather was nice, we stayed outside; when it was not, we went inside. Once it became dark, we were required to be inside our barracks. At night, we tried to sleep, but since our only bed was a concrete floor, sleeping was difficult. Throughout the day, I stayed as close as possible to my father and brother; I was careful, however, not to show by either words or gestures that we were related. On the assumption that being together gave their victims a better chance of survival, the Germans would separate family members. I did not want to give them that opportunity.

The food was meager—just enough to keep us from starving. In the morning after roll call, we were given an ersatz coffee made from something like charred wheat; for lunch, we had watery vegetable soup; and in the evening, we were given a slice of bread, or something resembling bread, and some margarine. Occasionally, we got some jelly or horse meat.

The soup was brought from the main kitchen in huge containers carried on poles by eight prisoners. We each had a metal cup, and sometimes a prisoner would try to dip his cup into the pot while the soup was being transported. If caught, he was badly beaten. And yet, some prisoners were so driven by hunger that they were willing to chance a beating for some extra food. If you were lucky, or if the Kapo especially liked you, you received soup dipped from the bottom of the pot, where the vegetables lay. I believe that Nonek tried to help me in this way. What I can tell you for certain is that we were always hungry.

The sanitation was primitive. In our camp, there was a large, dark building with water and toilets. The toilets were nothing more than long wooden benches with holes in them; they were public and dirty, and they stunk. Defecating was difficult. The facilities for washing consisted of long pipes with holes, out of which ran cold, dirty water. Without soap, towels, or paper, it was difficult to stay clean, but we tried. Staying clean and trying to look as good as possible was one of the few ways we had of affirming our humanity and of resisting German efforts to demoralize us.

Mostly, we waited to be sent to another camp to work. Often civilians, accompanied by SS, would come looking for workers. After we had been in Auschwitz about two weeks, some Germans came to our camp seeking prisoners who had worked in the metal factories in Lodz to go and work in Germany. My brother was among those chosen. He and the others who

were selected were separated from us and quarantined in a special barracks. I was able to talk to him through the wall, and he told me that the
food was better and that they were being treated well. It seemed to me that
he was fortunate. Shortly after he was quarantined, my brother left.[8] Now I
was alone with my father.

After my brother left, I had several chances to go to Germany to work
as a mason or a farmer. Anxious as I was to leave Auschwitz, I did not
volunteer. I was determined to remain with Father. I would leave only when
he did and with him.

Following a chilling event that occurred on the evening of Yom Kippur,
our search for work became increasingly urgent.[9] That night, the Germans,
who seemed to take pleasure in celebrating our holy days with extra cruel-
ties, descended on our camp. They were looking for seven hundred boys to
gas. With great risk to his life, Nonek grabbed me, put me under his bed,
and covered me with a blanket. For what seemed like hours, I stayed in my
hiding place. I could hear the boys—some were my friends—crying and
pleading as they were being led away. Lying there and listening to them
was unbearable.

Father did not know that Nonek had hidden me, and so he assumed
that I had been taken away with the other boys. When I came out of hiding
in the morning, he was delirious. He embraced me as closely as he possibly
could and exclaimed, "This is hell. We must get out of here." Desperately
we began to seek work, any work that would take us away from Auschwitz.
Two days later, when a call came for men to work in Germany, we volunteered, and soon we were in an truck headed out of Auschwitz. As we were
leaving, we passed by the women's camp. There, I saw women crawling
on all fours; they barely looked like human beings. I feel certain that they
were victims of some of Mengele's medical experiments.

The truck took us to a train that was filled with prisoners. We did not
know where we were headed but since the men in the transport appeared
to be in good condition, we felt confident that we were not going to the gas
chambers. Rather than being fearful—as Father said, "Nothing could be
worse than Auschwitz,"—I was mainly curious as to where we were going.
After a journey of two or three days, I would find out. Unfortunately, my
subsequent experiences would dwarf the horror that I had experienced at
Auschwitz. But I did not know that then. All I felt was relief at having survived Auschwitz, and thankfulness that I was still with my father.

1. Paul Berben, *Dachau, 1933-1945: The Official History* (London: Norfolk Press, 1975), 96. Berben states that conditions on the deportation trains were especially bad during the final year of the war due to Allied bombing of the train tracks and the increased demands of the army. On page 97, Berber includes several descriptions by survivors and witnesses of the deportation trains that arrived at Dachau; among them is the following:

    > A train left Compiegné in France on 2nd July 1944 and arrived at Dachau on 5th July in the early afternoon. The train left at 9:45 a.m. with 2,521 men on board, 100 in each goods truck. Ventilation was provided by two skylights measuring 2 ft 6 ins by 1 ft 8 ins and blocked with barbed wire. Very soon the worst had happened; caused by the exceptional heat of that summer's day, the long halts under the blazing sun, the overcrowding and the lack of water. There were scenes of delirium, men were maddened and killed each other. By the end, in Dr. Rohmer's truck for example, the 24 survivors were sleeping on the corpses: in two or three hours 74 of their colleagues had died of heat, asphyxia and thirst. The 'death train' reached Dachau with 1,537 survivors at 1.22 p.m. on the 5th of July. One single trainload had killed 984 men!

2. Hilberg, *The Destruction of the European Jews*, 2:428.

3. The estimate of the number of persons murdered at Auschwitz varies. Hilberg, *Destruction*, gives the number of 1,000,000; "Auschwitz," *Holocaust Encyclopedia*, says 1,100,000. The highest figure that I have seen is 2,000,000; this is in Botwinick, *A History of the Holocaust*, 192.

4. Morris's mother and sisters survived the selection at Auschwitz and were sent to Stutthof, a large work camp located in a marshy area in northern Poland, about twenty-two miles east of Danzig [Gdansk] and a few miles from the Baltic Sea. He has copies of the registration cards for all three at Stutthof. Although he knows that they did not survive the Holocaust, he does not know when, where, or how they died. He has heard from a survivor from Pabianice, who was in the camp with them, that they were among the many prisoners who were put on barges during the final days of the war when the camp was evacuated, and that the barge that they were on was sunk. Morris has not been able to verify this account. Now that the huge archive of Nazi records at Bad Arolsen has been opened, he is hoping that he may be able to learn for certain how they died.

5. The Sauna was located amidst the crematoria next to "Canada," the huge area for sorting and storing the clothes and other possessions of the victims.

6. Crowe, *Holocaust*, 258. On August 2, 1944, the Gypsy camp was liquidated; the 2,897 Gypsies who were still there were gassed at Birkenau. Prior to this, many Gypsies had died or been transferred to work camps in Germany.

7. Nonek survived the Holocaust and later immigrated to Australia.

8. Morris's brother Nachman [Nathan] was sent to a work camp in Germany; he survived the Holocaust. The brothers were reunited in 1946, and with the help of their father's eldest brother, Harry, they immigrated to the United States in 1949.

9. Yom Kippur, the holiest day of the Jewish year, occurred on September 27th in 1944.

Chapter 10

The Dachau Camps
(October 1944-April 1945)

From the early fall of 1944 through April 1945, I was a slave laborer in a number of different camps. It was in these camps that I endured the worst conditions, witnessed the worst horrors, and reached my lowest point. It was here that I watched my father die and then watched while a guard extracted his gold teeth. It was here that I received twenty-five lashes with a whip. During the months in the camps, there were times that I was certain that I would die, but through sheer luck and the unpredictability of the Nazi machine I continued to live. There were also times when I was ready to give up, when death seemed a welcome alternative. Through it all some instinct to survive kept me going; there was a fire in my belly that would not let me give up. Morris Glass

In the early autumn of 1944, Morris left Auschwitz in a cattle car headed for Germany, where he was being sent to help build factories to produce weapons for the Germans. Included among those weapons was the Messerschmitt jet, the Nazis' answer to the Allied bombers that by 1944 were pounding Germany virtually unopposed. The work was urgent. The new factories that were being built underground were incomplete, and, most relevant to Morris's experience, manpower was short. The Nazis' solution to this crisis was to bring in prisoners of various classifications and nationalities, including the few Jews who were still alive, to construct and man the factories. Among them were Morris and his father. Their fate was not unique. Millions of people, especially during the final years of the war, were forced to work in industries throughout the Third Reich.[1]

The Nazis' program of annihilating the Jews was one of the reasons for the extreme labor shortage. Included in their frenzy of extermination were millions of Jews who worked in war-related industries—clearly, the economic utility of the Jews was subordinate to the Nazis' goal of racial purity. Finally, in 1944, with the Soviets advancing from the east and Allied bombers pulverizing the industrial areas of northern Germany, the Ruhr, and the Rhine Valley, the Nazis decided to postpone their ideological commitment to destroy all Jews. Instead, they turned to the "remnant" of surviving Jews to help rescue Germany from defeat.

While this nod to pragmatism did not save the Third Reich, it did offer some Jews a chance to survive. For Morris, this decision was critical. It partially explains why the factories in Lodz were permitted to continue producing until the last summer of the war. This extra time in Lodz meant that Morris had a little more time to grow older and bigger before he was deported. The manpower shortage also may have saved him from being gassed when he arrived at Auschwitz. In addition, being deported late also meant that Morris had better odds of surviving in the work camps than the prisoners who had been in them longer.

Morris and his father were assigned to camps in the Dachau system, which by 1944 included the original camp at Dachau plus some 123 sub-camps.[2] Dachau is located about 12 miles northwest of Munich in the region of southern Germany known as Bavaria. The sub-camps were scattered all around this area in locations close to the factories, quarries, and construction sites where the inmates worked. Although the sub-camps were separated geographically from Dachau, they were connected administratively, and the workers assigned to them were shuffled around among the various camps. For example, in the seven months that Morris was an inmate in this system, he was in five different camps, in one of them twice.

Because it is difficult to keep track of Morris' whereabouts, below is a chronological list of the camps where he was imprisoned, along with his estimate of the dates when he was at each. The dates in brackets reflect information that was included in the records kept by the Nazis. These records are not complete. Also, sometimes they give an exact date, and other times they just indicate the month.

Kaufering IX, late September through mid-October.[3] [A photo of
    Morris's registration form is at the end of the chapter.]

Kaufering IV, mid-October through early November.

Kaufbeuren, November until mid-January, 1945. [Arrival date 11-9-
    1944.]

Dachau (the main camp), several weeks beginning at the end of
    January through mid-February 1945.

Mühldorf, mid-February through the end of March. [Arrival date,
    2-21, 1945.]

Kaufering IV, end of March until about April 26, when Morris was put
    on a train headed for Austria. Morris had been imprisoned in this
    camp earlier. (Kaufering IV was liberated by the U.S. Army on
    April 27.)

Although economic necessity may have saved Morris and other Jewish
workers from the gas chambers, these prisoners were nevertheless considered expendable. As a result, the conditions in which they lived and worked
were abominable. If the eleven Kaufering camps are representative of conditions in all of the Dachau sub-camps, then the conditions in these camps
were especially horrific, and the death toll was high.[4]

In some of the Dachau sub-camps, the barracks were built partially
underground so as to make them less visible to Allied bombers; as a result,
they were damp and muddy. Some of the barracks had no floors except
for wood planks. These planks also served as beds for the inmates. The
sanitary facilities were few and crude. There were perhaps two or three
toilets for a whole camp and a pipe with holes in it for washing. The camps
were infested with fleas and lice, and infectious diseases like dysentery,
typhus, and typhoid were rampant. The food was meager, and hunger was
a constant. One set of clothing was the rule, and there was no issue of extra
clothes for the cold winter months. Although the camps and places of work
were staffed by the SS and their auxiliaries, the sites where the prisoners
worked were controlled by either government agencies or private companies like I .G. Farben and the Bavarian Motor Works or, as it is better
known, BMW. Both of these companies are still in operation.

The work was hard labor, often in underground construction sites with
little ventilation or regard for safety. The hours were long, and the prisoners usually had to walk several miles to and from work. In addition, they
often had to stand outside for hours during the roll call. Most of the time
that Morris was in these camps, it was winter, and, as he puts it, "Bavarian

winters are brutal." It is no wonder that the death rate in the camps was high. These camps were known as "*Vernichtung durch Arbeit*" [annihilation through work]. They were places where the inmates were literally worked to death.

When I left Auschwitz, I was once again in a cattle car. Unlike the journey there, when I was with all of my family, I was now alone with my father. I was indeed grateful to be with him, and I was determined not to be parted from him. Although conditions in the cattle car were horrible, my outlook was good. I was not as fearful as I had been on the train from Lodz. In fact, I was happy, I might even say ecstatic, to be out of Auschwitz.

Our destination was a small camp called Kaufering IX that was a part of a complex of eleven camps near the town of Kaufering.[5] It was a new camp and our transport may have been one of the first to arrive there. It was here that I was registered and given my number, 112280. This is a number that I will never forget! Because of the mix of nationalities in the camps, I learned to say it in five languages: Yiddish, Polish, Hungarian, German, and French. My number was imprinted on a white band that was sewn on my jacket—I wore the same jacket for seven months.

Kaufering IX was a small camp, and in comparison to Auschwitz it was primitive. The barracks were built so that most of the building was underground; this meant that we had to go down several steps to enter. All you could see of the barracks from the outside was the V-shaped roof; supposedly, this would make it more difficult for Allied bombers to spot them. Along each of the walls there was a huge bench or shelf where we slept. The toilets and washing facilities were inadequate and unsanitary.

We did not work inside the camp or, for that matter, in any of the other camps where I was placed. Rather, each day we walked several miles to the work site and then several miles back. During the approximately four weeks that my father and I were there, we were assigned to an assortment of tasks most of which were related to constructing a small airfield. We hauled in stones to build roads and lumber to construct buildings. Other prisoners who were not Jewish did the actual construction; we were forbidden to talk to them. Fortunately, a couple of times I was included among groups of teenagers who were sent to work on nearby farms. Usually, the farmers gave us good soup, and we could bring some potatoes back to the camp. This was a lucky break.

The SS commander of this camp, a man named Hoffmann, was the most decent commander I had anywhere. He hardly beat anyone. Compared to the SS at Auschwitz, Hoffmann was a huge improvement. After the war, a number of prisoners testified at his trial to the effect that he had treated them decently. These testimonies probably saved him from the gallows.[6] After we had been at Kaufering IX for a few weeks, Hoffmann was transferred to another camp. He asked me to accompany him. The work would have been comparatively easy—cleaning SS barracks and washing and ironing uniforms. Going with him would have been a huge break for me, but I would not leave my father, and so I said no.

Shortly after Hoffmann left, Father and I were transferred to another camp, Kaufering IV. (In April 1945, I would be reassigned to this camp.) It was a large camp with prisoners of many nationalities—French, Greek, and a lot of Hungarians. There were also prisoners with a variety of classifications, including some Jehovah's Witnesses. Being with such a mix of people was a new experience for me. We were there maybe two weeks doing some temporary jobs. Then we were transferred to Kaufbeuren. It was at Kaufbeuren that I was exposed to the full horror of the Holocaust. There is no question that it was the worst camp that I was in. My stay there was an unending nightmare.

We arrived at Kaufbeuren around the beginning of November, just as the harsh Bavarian winter was beginning—it was freezing. I shiver even now when I think of the cold.[7] Located some 59 miles southwest of Dachau, this camp was not part of the Kaufering complex of camps. Like them, it was a new camp that had been established to furnish slave laborers for the Nazi war machine. Kaufbeuren was notorious for the brutal treatment of the prisoners confined there. I can attest that it deserves to be labeled a Vernichtung [annihilation] camp. Although I do not know the exact figures, I would estimate that of the approximately 750 inmates who were there after we arrived only about 100 were still alive when the camp was liquidated some two and a half months later.

Because the camp was in a forest that provided camouflage, the barracks at Kaufbeuren, unlike those at the two previous camps, were above ground, and they had triple bunks on the side walls for sleeping. So the living conditions were a little improved. The routine was similar: wake up before dawn, go to roll call and then drink ersatz coffee, march some three to four miles to work, work all day with watery soup at noon, march back, eat a meal of bread which was a greenish color and some margarine and maybe some horse meat or imitation jelly, and then go to sleep. The conditions were so inhumane that after eating, we just wanted to fall into the bunk. It was dark when we marched to work, and it was dark when we

*returned. Always it was freezing, and we had nothing to protect ourselves
from the cold except our flimsy prison outfits. The only day we had off from
work was every other Sunday.*

*At Kaufbeuren, we worked constructing a huge underground factory
that was to produce various armaments like guns, tanks and locomo-
tives. It was an enormous place, like a little city. It even had a railroad
track running through it. The work was punishing. With picks and shovels,
Father and I hacked dirt out of the frozen ground; we then carried it away
in wheelbarrows. It was exhausting work, especially for two city people
who had never done any physically demanding labor. Furthermore, if we
did not work fast enough, there was always a guard nearby ready to hit us.
Almost every day some prisoners were left behind to be buried. One would
think that, since laborers were so scarce, the SS would have treated us better. Instead, it seemed as though the Germans, in an effort to make up for
the shortage, forced the few workers that they had to work even harder.[8]
With so many of us dying, the Germans must have become increasingly
shorthanded.*

*Whether at work or in the camp, the guards did not need an excuse to
beat us. Using shovels, gun butts, canes, or their hands they would beat
us half to death for the smallest thing, and they seemed to get tremendous
pleasure from doing so. As a group, the worst guards were the Ukrainians.
They were more anti-Semitic than the Germans and more brutal.*

*The most vicious and sadistic guards that I encountered anywhere
during the Holocaust were August Richard Ruhnke, the SS officer who was
the camp commander at Kaufbeuren , and his prisoner assistant, Albert
Talens. Ruhnke was maybe in his fifties. He was short and very stocky—
he was built pretty solidly. Dressed in his SS uniform, with a death's head
adorning the hat and collar and medals covering the jacket, Ruhnke would
stride around the camp accompanied by his ever-present German shepherd. He always carried a big, black cane that he would use to inflict pain
whenever he could. At roll call when the number of sick and dead prisoners
was reported to him, he was never satisfied. "Not enough, not enough," he
would scream. One bitterly cold Sunday near Christmas, we were standing at roll call when suddenly Ruhnke ordered us to take off our shirts.
One Hungarian, a man named Lazlo, had placed a piece of paper from a
cement bag on his chest to help him keep warm. At the sight of the paper,
Ruhnke went crazy. He ordered Lazlo to step out and then proceeded to
beat him to death—because of an old cement bag. I swore that if I survived,
I would bring this man to justice. I had the great pleasure of attending his*

trial and testifying against him. He was hanged on November 14, 1947, at Landsberg Prison.[9]

As bad as Ruhnke was, his assistant, Albert Talens, was worse. Talens, himself a prisoner, was designated as the commander inside the camp; his title was Lageraltester [Head of the Camp]. Unlike Ruhnke who lived outside the camp, Talens lived in the camp and so he was always with us. He was born in Germany, but he had moved to the Netherlands. He was classified as a criminal. I can tell you that he was one rotten human being. Talens was intensely interested in prisoners with gold fillings. I have been told that when he was captured by the Americans after the war, he had two pockets full of gold teeth. This is the man who killed my father, and it was he who pulled out my father's gold teeth. It was also he who whipped me after my father died. I also testified at his trial in Maastricht, Netherlands in 1986. Unfortunately, because of technicalities, he was not convicted.*[10]

The inhumane treatment from the guards, the cold, the hard labor, and the meager rations combined to deplete our numbers. As Christmas neared—I knew this because I could hear the guards singing "O Tannenbaum" ("Oh Christmas Tree")—there were so few of us alive that the SS put all of the prisoners in one barrack, which could hold about three hundred people. By this time we were in such bad condition that, knowing that some would not make it through the night, we would say our good-byes before we went to sleep.

Among those in terrible shape was my father. Father grew weaker and weaker until he could no longer go to work. Talens told him to report to the sick area, but Father, knowing that the sick bay was just one step from the grave and that one rarely lasted over twenty-four hours there, refused to go. Holding to the hope that he would soon feel better, Father stayed behind in the block when the rest of us went to work. While we were away, Talens would beat him. He would beat him below the heart and lungs in such a way that there were few visible marks; internally, however, there was much damage. I promise you, the Germans knew how to do this. They were champions at beating people.

When I returned from work and lay next to him in the bunk, Father would mumble about the beatings. I was in terrible condition myself—I was cold, hungry, and exhausted. Ashamed as I am to tell this, I would simply fall asleep. I don't know what he said. Sadly, I was not much comfort to my dying father. About a week after the beatings began, I woke up one morning and saw Talens and some of his helpers dragging my father from the bunk. I followed them and watched as they took him to a shed where, while *his body was still warm, they extracted his gold teeth. My father was barely dead.*

Wanting to pay my final respects to my father, I volunteered for the burial Kommando [work group]. The burial team consisted of four men who, holding a blanket with several skeletal bodies in it, marched about a half mile to a pit in the woods where, without any ceremony, they dropped the bodies, and then sprinkled chlorine on them. That day we had to make several trips as there was a pile of bodies held over from the past few days. Among the bodies was that of Lazlo. It took two or three hours—there were a lot of corpses.[11]

When I returned from burying the dead, I was greeted by Talens. He was enraged because I had not reported for work—didn't I know that the Germans were shorthanded? Furthermore, I had not asked his permission to help with the burials. Because of my actions, he decreed that I would receive fifty lashes with a whip when everyone returned from work—making all of the prisoners witness a whipping was standard procedure. When the time came, I had to pull down my pants and lean over a table. Luckily for me, at this point, Ruhnke appeared and thankfully ordered, "Only twenty-five; he is underage." And then the whipping began. One, two, three—after that I went numb; I no longer felt anything. I still have the marks from it. I guess I will go to the grave with them. That was the price that I paid to bury my father.

When the ordeal was over, a few of my fellow prisoners pulled me off the table and took me to a bunk, where they cared for me. They found rags and dampened them with snow and put them on my behind. I lay there in terrible pain. The next morning, with the help of my friends, I managed to walk to work—fear took me there, and fear brought me back. Fear is a fierce motivator. That night, my friends once again put cold rags on my cuts. Due to their care and my own determination, somehow I made it. A few days after the whipping, the Germans celebrated Christmas, and we had a day off. This was a true gift. Never have I been so thankful for a Christian holiday!

My father's death and my whipping constitute the lowest point of my life. I almost lost the will to live. But yet, there was a spark inside me that kept me going— some animal instinct that would not let me give up. And so, with little left but memories, I moved from one day to the next. Fortunately, it was not too long before Kaufbeuren was liquidated, and I and the "remnant of the remnant," maybe about one hundred prisoners, were transported to the main camp at Dachau. This probably occurred dur-

ing the second or third week of January.

Hard as it is to believe, being at Dachau was a respite from the ordeal of Kaufbeuren. The weeks that I spent there probably made it possible for me to outlive the Holocaust. I am thankful for them. Although I do not know why we were sent to Dachau, I believe that the Germans must have been so desperate for workers that they decided to give us some time to recuperate in the hope that we could resume working for them. This is only a guess, but based on the labor shortage and on the treatment that we received in the few weeks we were there, it makes sense. My first few hours at Dachau, however, were ominous and did not lend themselves to positive thoughts about the future.

Once off the train, we trudged to the camp where in front of the entrance we were greeted by four gallows with prisoners hanging from them. I don't know how long the bodies had been hanging there, but that was our welcome. Once inside, we were marched straight towards the crematoria. I could smell the stench of burning bodies—it was a smell that I knew well. I was positive that this was the end for all of us. Here we were, some one hundred Jews, all of whom were half-sick and could scarcely walk. Death seemed a certainty. We were taken to the showers, where we were ordered to undress and to hand over our clothes. As we entered the showers, we said our good-byes and prayed. But instead of gas, out came water! I was stunned. I couldn't believe it. Water, it was really water! A huge sigh of relief went up. We simply could not believe that it was water. We were joyful. After the showers, we were given back our uniforms. They were damp from having been washed and disinfected. This was wonderful; it meant we would have a brief vacation from the lice and fleas that tormented us. I received the precious shoes that I had worn since leaving Lodz. We were then taken to our barracks, where there were bunks, and we were given soup with real vegetables like carrots and potatoes, not just potato peels! I couldn't believe it.

My experience at Dachau turned out to be very different from Kaufbeuren and the other camps I had been in. Not only were the circumstances better, but it had a different atmosphere. The prisoners were different; many were political prisoners who had been at Dachau for a long time. The work was easy. We worked only occasionally, mainly cleaning up along the railroad tracks after the Allies had bombed them. Mostly, we rested. The guards rarely beat us, and when they occasionally did, the beatings were mild, especially compared to the sadistic beatings at Kaufbeuren. Honestly, we got a reprieve! Also, while at Dachau, we could hear the bombing around Munich.[12] This was a good sign; it lifted our spirits. It gave us hope that the Germans were retreating and that the Allies were advancing toward us.

The worst part of being at Dachau was the morning roll calls, which went on for what seemed like, and may well have been, hours. It was the height of winter and we had nothing to protect us from the cold except each other. So we stood at attention and froze. I can remember crying because I was so cold. I remember how my good friend Libel would try to keep me warm by standing as close to me as possible and sneaking his arm around me. He tried hard to help and to encourage me. His efforts brought warmth to my soul if not to my body.

But all in all the four weeks that we were at Dachau, improbable as it may seem, were comparatively easy. If the aim of the Germans was to refuel us so that we could go back to work, then they succeeded with me. With my body rested and my spirit energized by the possibility of liberation, I was in better condition to survive, both physically and mentally, when I left Dachau than when I arrived.

According to the records from Dachau, on February 21, 1945, I was sent from there to the Mühldorf Camp, another Dachau sub-camp 51.5 miles east of Dachau. As I recollect, I was part of a group of about three hundred prisoners who were transferred there. Mühldorf, like the first three camps I had been in, had recently been constructed to house slave labor-ers. The factory where we worked was involved in the production of the Messerschmitt jet. Conditions at Mühldorf were similar to the other camps I had been in, and so were the routine and the food. As to our treatment, some of the guards were decent, and some were brutal. Almost all of them were badly wounded and were no longer able to fight. Most were missing a leg, an arm, or an eye. I worked in a quarry with a lot of other people; we put rocks on lorries and moved sand. The work was hard but not impos-sible. I didn't much care what I was doing; all I could think about was making it out alive.

The unique aspect of Mühldorf was that it was adjacent to a small air-field. Only a fence separated the camp from the field, and our barracks had a red cross painted on the roof to protect them from Allied bombers. This location gave us a front-row seat to watch some air combat. It also gave us insight into how the war was progressing.

We could see the German planes coming and going, but, more impor-tantly, we could watch as the American B-29s flew over by the hundreds. My God, what an incredible sight! Seeing these planes gave us an enor-

mous lift. Usually the Allied planes just flew over the airfield on their way to bomb railroads and railroad stations—or at least this is what we thought they were doing. The German planes never flew up to challenge them—I presume because there were too few of them.

Twice, I watched when the Allies attacked the airfield in an effort to disable the German planes. What a sight! The first time was in the middle of the night. First, the Allies dropped flares in order to see the German planes and then they swooped down and used machine guns to hit the planes. When they hit a German plane, we were so happy. It was hard to contain our joy. A few days later, they came again, this time on a Sunday afternoon when we were not working. Once again, they flew in low and used machine guns to hit the planes. We prisoners rushed into a hole that served as a bomb shelter and watched the action. We counted the planes and whispered to each other. We were so excited! We were convinced that the war must be almost over. Unfortunately, a few of the prisoners were killed by stray bullets.

After about a month at Mühldorf, I became sick with dysentery, a nasty disease that in the camps was often a death sentence.[13] Now, my hopes of surviving the war were in jeopardy. I desperately wanted to get well. I also wanted to avoid the sick bay, so I tried to cure myself. A friend told me that if I boiled the needles of an evergreen tree and drank the broth it might help. I traded my rations for some needles, but I did not improve. Finally, when I was just too weak to work, I reluctantly went to the sick area. Here, I heard about another remedy that required eating burnt potatoes. To get them, a sick friend and I risked our lives by sneaking back into the regular camp to exchange our rations for the precious potatoes. For some reason—I doubt that it was the burnt potatoes—I started to feel better. Sadly, my friend died.

As soon as I was well, I wanted to return to the main camp where, I was sure, my chances of surviving were much better. I went to the commander, puffed out my chest, saluted, and exclaimed that I was cured and wanted to go back to work. He looked at me, shook his head, and told me that typhoid, which is extremely contagious and deadly, had been discovered in the sick area. As a consequence, no one would be allowed to leave. I was stuck in the sick bay, and my outlook looked grim. Then, orders came that the sick bay at Mühldorf was to be liquidated and that everyone there was to be deported to Kaufering IV. Kaufering IV, one of the camps where I had been imprisoned in the fall, now functioned exclusively as a typhoid camp where the sick from other Dachau camps were sent. Now, the outlook for me looked even grimmer.

When, around the first of April, I left Mühldorf in a cattle car full of sick and dying people, my heart was heavy. I was certain that we were being sent to our deaths; no other conclusion seemed possible. I said to myself, "This is it." Once again, I repeated the prayers for the dying and said my good-byes. Then I fell asleep. Amazingly, when I woke up in the morning, I was still alive, and we were at Kaufering IV. I'll never understand why the Nazis went to the trouble of sending that car full of half-dead Jews to a sick camp. If you could have seen us, you would have known that we were incapable of any further work. It just didn't make sense. I can only guess that they were just that desperate for laborers.

Even though I had fully recovered from the dysentery and was relatively healthy, I was placed in a block with all the typhoid cases. For weeks, I lay next to people who had typhoid, some of whom died in the night. Amazingly, I escaped being infected. I have heard that about 90 percent of those sent to Kaufering IV died. It seemed to me that the larger guys had a harder time with typhoid than the smaller ones. This is a purely personal observation, but I am small and I did not catch it. Actually, except for my bout with dysentery, I was not sick in the ghetto or the camps; this is another example of how fortunate I was.

Because I was among the few prisoners who were in fairly decent condition, one of the camp doctors, himself a prisoner, made me his assistant. Helping the doctor was not pleasant work; my reward was an extra ration of bread. The worst task that I had was putting salve on open sores, sores which swarmed with hundreds of lice. It was a repugnant task.

While helping the doctor, I witnessed many gruesome scenes. One day, we entered a shack where some prisoners were boiling and eating the buttocks of dead inmates, an act punishable by death. The doctor immediately stopped them. It was a horrible thing for me to see, and to this day, chills run up and down my spine when I think about it. Although I have heard of other instances of cannibalism in the camps, this was the only time that I saw it. I do know that hunger can drive a person to do terrible things.

At the typhoid camp, we often heard the sound of gunfire that, as the weeks passed, seemed to grow closer and closer. As the Allies drew nearer, I and some of the other able-bodied prisoners were given the grisly task of ridding the camp of corpses. Our job was to pick up the bodies lying around the camp and along the roads and dump them in a pit. Finally, one day when it seemed that the Allies were only six or seven kilometers away, we were told to put the bodies in a pile. Then, Germans in protective clothing and gas masks came, poured gas on the bodies, and proceeded to burn them and everything else in the camp. They knew the Americans were coming, and they were trying to hide the atrocities that they had committed. The Germans then ordered those prisoners who could walk to march to the railroad tracks. Shortly thereafter, we were loaded onto a huge train.

After the war, I learned that on April 27, shortly after the train departed, the camp was liberated by the U.S. Army.[14] The Americans who liberated Kaufering IV took photographs, gave testimonies, and wrote memoirs that amply document the filth, the dead bodies, and the emaciated condition of the few remaining inmates.[15] The Americans were so appalled and enraged that they ordered the German civilians in the neighboring town of Hurlach to come to the camp and carry the remaining bodies to a mass grave.[16]

Another thing that I learned later was just how lucky I was. If I had stayed at Mühldorf as I had wanted to, I would have been forced on a death march. In my weak condition, it is doubtful that I could have survived. Surviving the train was difficult enough.[17]

1. "In August 1944, more than 7,500,000 non-German workers were registered as working in the Reich; the overwhelming majority were forced laborers." USHMM, "Forced Labor in Depth," *Holocaust Encyclopedia*, www.ushmm.org/wlc/article.php?lang=en&ModuleId=10007326 (accessed on September 8, 2010).

2. The number 123 seems to be the figure that is most accepted. However, Paul Berben, in *Dachau, the Official History* (London: The Norfolk Press), 89, gives a higher figure. He states, "Dachau had about 165 outside *Kommandos* at the end of the War." Because the Dachau camps were opened and closed at different times, because they were designated by different names, and because some included separate men's and women's camps, it is difficult to find exact agreement as to the number.

   The following information about the Mühldorf Camp, where Morris stayed during February and March 1945, illustrates the problem of counting: "The Mettenheim camp held some 2,000 inmates, a nearby women's camp 2,500 persons, the 'forest camps' (Waldlager) about 2,250 male and female inmates, while two other camps held a total of 550 persons." USHMM, "Mühldorf," *Holocaust Encyclopedia*, http://www.ushmm.org/wlc/en/article.php?ModuleId=10006172 (accessed on September 8, 2010).

   Although I have no figures that show how many prisoners were in the Dachau system when Morris arrived, USHMM, "Dachau," *Holocaust Encyclopedia*, states that at the time of liberation, April 26, 1945, there "were 67,665 registered prisoners in Dachau and its sub-camps; more than half of this number were in the main camp. Of these, 43,350 were categorized as political prisoners, while 22,100 were Jews, with the remainder falling into various other categories."

(http://www.ushmm.org/wlc/en/article.php?ModuleId=10005214 (accessed on September 8, 2010.)

3. There is a slight discrepancy between Morris's recollection as to when he left Auschwitz and arrived at Kaufering IX, and the Dachau records. Morris recollects that he left several days after Yom Kippur which occurred on September 27 in 1944. The registration form at Kaufering IX gives the date of his arrival as September 29, 1944.

4. The eleven camps near the city of Kaufering, which is located about forty-two miles southwest of Dachau, were referred to as Kaufering I-XI. The son of one of the American soldiers who liberated these camps has created an excellent web site, "Kaufering," that is devoted to information about them. According to this site,

    > In just ten months of operation, more than 30,000 prisoners, mostly Jews, were imprisoned in the eleven (Kaufering) camps. Half did not live to see liberation. The camps were in operation for around ten months. 14,500 died in just 10 months. 31,951 died at Dachau in 12 years ...the inhumanity, suffering, death, disease, and torture is considered to be among the worst of all Nazi concentration camps.

    Joe Kleon, "Kaufering," http://www.kaufering.com/overview.html (accessed October 18, 2010).

5. The town of Kaufering is close to Landsberg where Hitler was imprisoned for eight months in 1924 during which time he wrote *Mein Kampf.*

6. I have been unsuccessful in locating information about Hoffmann and his trial and sentencing. One basic problem is that I do not know how his name was spelled nor what his first name was, and Hoffmann is a very common name in Germany. I did locate information about a Walter Hoffmann who was tried by the U.S. Army Courts in Europe (1945-1948) as part of the "Dachau Trials" [Case Number: US324 Case No. 000-50-2-41 (US vs Gottlob Beck et al]. This Walter Hoffman was given a sentence of two years (st.450503).

7. This camp was also known as Camp Riederloh because it was located in a forest outside of the village of Riederloh. This town was near the larger city of Kaufbeuren where the work site was located.

8. USHMM. "Forced Labor: In Depth." *Holocaust Encyclopedia*, http://www. ushmm.org/wlc/en/article.php?ModuleId=10007326 (accessed on September 8, 2010). This article discusses the inflexibility of the camp commanders, even when they were instructed from above to improve conditions for the workers in the camps:

    > As the tide of war turned against Germany in 1942-1943, the need for labor increased and the ability of the Germans to extract laborers from the occupied Soviet Union decreased due to military defeat. The concentration camp administration sought to induce camp commandants to take measures to prolong the lives of their forced laborers, who in 1944 were becoming a more precious commodity. Nevertheless, the camp commandants found it difficult to change ingrained and ideologically reinforced habits of treating

prisoners in such a way as to increase the rate of death; for the SS, the prisoners remained 'the enemy behind the wire.'

9. August Richard Ruhnke (9/9/1900-11/14/1947) was tried by a U.S. Army Court on April 16-18, 1947 and sentenced to death by hanging; he was hanged on November 14, 1947. The charge against him was the "Deliberate killing of prisoners (especially those with gold teeth)... [and] mishandling of prisoners" at the Kaufbeuren Camp. Transcript of his trial from April 16 through 18 by the U.S. Army Courts, File Number: US356.

10. Albert Talens was put on trial in April 1983 in Maastricht, Netherlands, on the charge of crimes against humanity. Morris and several other former inmates of Kaufbeuren testified against him. Morris recounted his father's death; several others described Talens' role in the beating of a prisoner who had wrapped cement bags around his body. (This is the same incident that Morris describes in which a prisoner was forced to strip outside in the freezing cold.) The Dutch court decided that the charges were not proven, and Talens was released. There were lengthy reports of his trial in at least four Dutch newspapers (De Limburger, De Telegraaf, Het Parool and Algemeen Dagblad); these include testimony by Morris. Short synopses also appeared in The Times (London) and the New York Times. The article in Het Parool includes a sketch of the witnesses, including Morris.

11. "The mass grave where my father and hundreds of other prisoners were buried was located years after the war mainly through the efforts of a son of one of the prisoners who was buried there." Morris Glass

A marker has been erected there to commemorate the site.

12. A few months after the war, Morris went to Munich where he saw firsthand the work of the Allied bombers. "In Munich there was hardly a block that wasn't destroyed. I mean there were chimneys in the thousands. It was unbelievable."

13. Dysentery, a disease of the intestinal tract, is caused by unsanitary conditions. It is an awful disease marked by bloody diarrhea, and in the camps, it often resulted in death. The filth in the camps furnished a perfect breeding ground for this disease, and also for typhus and typhoid. All three diseases were rampant in the camps especially toward the end of the war.

14. Kaufering IV was liberated on April 27 by the 7th Army, 12th Armored Division. It received help from soldiers in the 101St Airborne Division who arrived on April 28.

15. USHMM. "Kaufering-Photographs," *Holocaust Encyclopedia*, http://www. ushmm.org/wlc/en/gallery_ph.php?ModuleId=10006171 (accessed on September 8, 2010). This site has numerous photographs of Kaufering IV at the time of liberation.

The "Kaufering" site also has numerous photographs. http://www.kaufering.com/overview.html (accessed October 18, 2010).

The site "Liberation of Kaufering IV Dachau Sub-camp," http://www.scrapbook-pages.com/DachauscrapbookDachauLiberation/KauferingIVLiberation.html (accessed October 20, 2010), states that Dr. Charles P. Larson, a U. S. Army doctor who examined 258 bodies, reported that 189 probably died of typhus or starvation, 86 had apparently been burned to death, 11 shot inside the camp and 17 more outside the camp. None died from poison gas.

Stephen Spielberg recreated the liberation of Kaufering IV in the television series, "Band of Brothers."

16. The site "Liberation of Kaufering," states, "The commandant Johann Baptist Eichelsdorfer was convicted by an American Military Tribunal at Dachau and sentenced to death. He was hanged at Landsberg Prison, only a few miles from the Kaufering IV Camp, on May 29, 1946." http://www.scrapbookpages.com/ DachauscrapBook/DachauLiberation/KauferingIVLiberation.html (accessed September 8, 2010).

17. While Morris considers that he was lucky not to have been on the death march from Mühldorf, being put on a train was often not an especially good alternative. The descriptions of some of the trains that were used to transport prisoners at the end of the war are horrifying.

USHMM, "Dachau," *Holocaust Encyclopedia*, http://www.ushmm.org/wlc/en/ article.php?ModuleId=10005214 (accessed on September 8, 2010). This site states that as the American soldiers neared the main camp at Dachau "they found more than 30 railroad cars filled with bodies brought to Dachau, all in an advanced state of decomposition."

USHMM, "The 45th Infantry Division," *Holocaust Encyclopedia*, http://www. ushmm.org/wlc/en/article.php?ModuleId=10006163http://www.ushmm.org/wlc/ en/article.php?ModuleId=10006163 (accessed on September 8, 2010). This site includes the following description:

> On April 28, the day before liberation, a train bearing about 40 or so railway cars arrived at the camp. It had left Buchenwald four weeks earlier on April 7 filled with more than 5,000 prisoners. With few provisions, almost 2,000 inmates died during the circuitous route that took them from Thuringia through Saxony to Czechoslovakia and into Bavaria. Their bodies were left behind in various locations throughout Germany. When U.S. troops arrived in Dachau on April 29, they found 2,310 additional corpses on the train. The 816 surviving prisoners were taken to barracks within the camp.

Morris's Registration Card at Dachau.

Chapter 11

The Final Episode

*The final episode in the saga of my survival was fraught with dan-
ger and filled with ecstasy. In less than a month, I experienced several
brushes with death and the jubilation of liberation. The last part of my
story begins and ends with departures. It begins with my departure from
the typhoid camp on a train bound for Austria and, if Himmler had had
his way, death. It ended with my departure from St. Ottelien, a hospital for survivors, on the back of a truck with soldiers from the Jewish
Brigade. All this occurred from the end of April to the end of May 1945.
During this same month, Hitler committed suicide, Germany surrendered,
the remaining camps were liberated, and the Holocaust was over.* Morris
Glass

The circumstances surrounding the liberation of the Dachau camps
during the final weeks of the war were confusing. The confusion was
partly the result of the geographical separation of the camps which made a
coordinated response to the Allied advance difficult. Another problem was
that the Nazis did not have a viable plan for what to do with the prisoners.
Himmler was sending orders not to let a single prisoner live. However,
to the commanders at the Dachau camps, there seemed to be no practical
way to comply with his directive. There were rumors circulating among
the prisoners that they were to be fed poisoned soup. Morris thought that
he was being sent to the Austrian border to be poisoned in this manner.[1]
Furthermore, there was a breakdown in communications between southern Germany and Berlin; in fact, the entire governmental structure was in
disarray.

All of these factors and more led to different scenarios in different places. Some of the prisoners were sent on "death marches" toward Austria. Some, like Morris, were put on trains headed toward Austria or Dachau. Others were marched to the main camp at Dachau and still others were marched away from Dachau. If it is difficult for the historian to understand what was happening during the last weeks of the war, then it must have been extraordinarily difficult for the prisoners themselves. Without a doubt, this was a time of confusion, anxiety, and fear for those in the camps. It is known that in the last days of the war, all inmates of the Kaufering camps except for the sick were evacuated. Some were marched to the main Dachau camp; others, like Morris, were put on trains headed for either Dachau or Austria.

Walking the half kilometer from Kaufering IV to the railroad tracks was no easy task for most of us. We walked as slowly as possible and as close to each other as possible in order to help those who were struggling—otherwise, they would have been shot. After we had waited several hours, a huge train appeared. It stretched as far as the eye could see and held thousands of people.[2] Because the cattle cars were full, my group was put in a coal car, where we were stacked like sardines, one on top of the other. Most were sick and burning with fever. People were dying all around me. Once again I thought, "This is the end." But now more than ever, I desperately wanted to live. I was certain that the war would end soon. Liberation seemed very near.

There were a number of signs that indicated that the days of the mighty Third Reich were numbered. The Allied guns sounded very close. I saw very young boys, maybe 14, 15, or 16 years old, manning huge anti-aircraft guns— a sure sign that the Germans were on their last leg. Furthermore, it was whispered that some of the SS guards had been heard to say that the surrender would be soon. I had listened to rumors for years, but I knew this one must be true. Unfortunately, we also heard troubling reports that we were being sent to the Tyrol Forest on the border between Germany and Austria to be fed poisoned soup. This was a rumor that I hoped was not true, but knowing the Nazis, I feared the worst. Thank God for Generals Patton, Eisenhower and Taylor, and all the others! It was because of their rapid advance that I never found out if there was truth to the poisoning rumor.

I'm not sure how many days I was on the train. At some point, we came under fire from American and British planes that were attacking German

anti-aircraft guns. In order to discourage the attack, the Germans deliberately parked our train next to the guns. The Allied planes were flying very
low—so low the pilots could see us. I know that they tried not to hit us, but
sometimes they did. Those of us in open cars lay there totally helpless, like
dead ducks. There were a lot of casualties. I saw people with missing arms
and legs and other terrible wounds. There was no one to care for them. All
of a sudden, I felt wet and warm. I thought, "Oh, no, after all these years,
I'm to be killed by my friends." When I recovered from my fright and I
checked myself, I was okay. What I had felt was hot water gushing from a
locomotive that had been punctured.

As a result of the Allied attack, our train was damaged and stalled,
and there were piles of dying people in my car and along the tracks. There
was confusion and panic everywhere. When I saw some SS fleeing into
the woods, I thought that I must be hallucinating, but then I realized that
the war just might be over. I decided that if the SS were leaving, then I too
would leave, and so I and four others rolled off the train. I said to them,
"It's a matter of hours. Our liberators must be very close. Let's walk toward the village," and off we went. One of my friends, Libel, had pneumo-
nia and was burning with fever. He was very sick, so we walked slowly.

We walked to a farm, where the family gave us food. Thinking that the
war must be over and that we were safe, we rested for several hours. But
our dream of freedom was soon ended when some German militia arrested
us. First, we were taken to a Wehrmacht officer who spoke kindly to us
and assured us that the war would be over shortly. We begged him to let
us go, but he said that he was under orders to detain all prisoners. Then,
the SS came and accused us of being spies who were running toward the
Americans. They wrote down our numbers and told us that we would be
executed in the morning. I don't know why they did not shoot us then, but
luckily for us they didn't. The SS took us to a wooded area where there were
hundreds of wounded and dying prisoners. We could hear them crying,
"Hear, O Israel," and pleading for help. Amidst all the suffering, it was
hard to think about oneself.

Nevertheless, knowing that the war was almost over, my friends and
I were determined to escape execution. Since the SS knew us only by the
numbers on our jackets, we exchanged our jackets for the jackets of dead
prisoners. Feeling protected by our new numbers, we slept through the
night. In the morning, after some SS gave us permission to get water for
the sick and dying, the five of us started to walk away from the camp. Just
as we started walking, the sky became very dark and rain started to come

down in sheets. With our movements shielded by the dark and the rain, we walked away from the SS as fast as we could. Finally, we met a farmer who took us in, gave us food, and hid us in his hayloft. While we were lying in the hay, we heard the SS come. They searched and searched, but they did not find us. When we went to sleep that night, we were aware that we had much to be grateful for.

When we awoke in the morning, we were greeted by the great news that there had been a radio announcement (which it turned out was incorrect) that Germany had surrendered. Our joy at this news was tempered by the worsening condition of Libel. We knew something had to been done imme-diately, or he would die. Seeing how sick Libel was, the farmer told us that there was a hospital only a kilometer away. It seemed once again that luck was with us.

Jauntily, we set out for the hospital. Believing that the war was over, that we were out of danger, and that there was a place nearby where Libel would be cared for, we were a happy group. Unfortunately, we had not walked far, when we learned that all was not well. The messenger of bad news was a hulking SS officer who was sitting on a motorcycle in the middle of the road, holding a machine gun. As we rounded the curve and saw him, I thought, "Oh, my God, what will we do." Somehow, I quickly came to my senses, calmly walked up to him, and told him that we were lost and wanted to go back to the train. He must have believed me because he gave us directions and let us go. We started walking as instructed, but as soon as the road curved, we raced into the forest.

We would have been happy to have stayed in the forest until we knew for certain that the SS had departed and that the war was really over, but Libel was very, very sick, and we had to get him to the hospital. We waited until dark and then set out once again. Covering the short distance to the hospital took a long time because every time we heard a car or any strange noise, we would jump back into the woods. Finally, we saw the lights of a large building. We went around the back, and I knocked on the door. It was opened by a nun. I didn't have to say anything; she just motioned us to come in. We had arrived at St. Ottilien, a Benedictine monastery, that had been converted into an SS hospital. We were now under the care of kindly nuns and monks, but we were not yet out of danger.

The nuns were so good to us. They gave us food and took our filthy prison clothes, which they burned. When I said, "I have one wish. I would like to take a bath," they took all of us to be bathed. And wonder of won-ders, there I was, I who had not had a real bath in years, in a bathtub with

soap, hot water, and a nun who came and scrubbed me. This was heaven!!!
I must have been in that tub for hours. After the bath, the monks gave us
new clothes, and then they whisked us away and hid us in a hayloft—it was
still an SS hospital. The monks told us that it was a matter of days until the
war would be over, and we would be free. In the meantime, we could stay
where we were, and they would bring us food.

A day or two later, the monks told us that the Americans were very
near, and since there might be some shooting, we should move to the base-
ment where it would be safer. We went to the basement. I found a box to
stand on so that I could see out of the window—I was not going to miss a
thing. Before long, I was rewarded with a view of an American tank coming
up the hill.

How can I describe the jubilation I felt when I first glimpsed that tank
flying an Americans flag? There is no way to describe the joy in my heart—
the joy of being free! I ran outside and embraced the first soldier I saw
and then another and another and another. I was happy beyond my ability
to describe it. I was free! I was free! I was free! A minute ago, I had been
a prisoner and hiding, and now I was free and hugging every American
soldier I could find. I just could not believe it.

I was then and I remain now very grateful to the American army for
giving me back my life and my freedom. My gratitude has no bounds. Every
time I see the stars and stripes, I am reminded of my debt to those soldiers
and to the American army.

On spotting us, one of the soldiers yelled out, "We need five beds im-
mediately. On his orders, we were taken into the hospital and everything
possible was done to help us. The Americans put us on a strict diet and
checked us every few hours. Because so many survivors had died from
overeating, they carefully supervised what and how much we ate. The
German SS doctors treated us politely and tried to help us—they said
they wanted to redeem themselves. Of course, the nuns and the monks
were wonderful. Much care was devoted to Libel. The Americans and the
Germans tried to save him, but he died shortly after we were liberated. To
lose him, especially after we were free, put a damper on our spirits, but
even his death could not destroy our joy.

Shortly after I was put in the hospital, the soldier who had ordered the
beds came to check on us. When he was giving the order, I thought that I
had heard him using some Jewish words, but I said, "No, no, Morris, you
are fantasizing." Well, I wasn't. It turned out that he was a Jewish guy from
Brooklyn. That made me so proud—one of my saviors was an American

Jew! Also among the American liberators was a black man; this was the first time that I had ever seen a black person except in the circus. My life was indeed full of new and wondrous things.

St. Ottelien was a perfect place for me to be. In addition to the hospital, it included a farm with cows and other animals, and wheat and potato fields. The bounty of nature and the serenity of the countryside buoyed my spirits, and with the good care that I was receiving, I improved rapidly.

Recognizing that this was an ideal place to recover, General Eisenhower decreed that St. Ottilien was to be a hospital for Jewish survivors. Within two or three weeks, there must have been a thousand of us there, all needing medical attention. The SS doctors were removed from the hospital and replaced by American doctors and by Jewish doctors who were themselves survivors. The Jews there, like survivors everywhere, were desperately seeking their loved ones. As soon as I met another survivor, I would immediately ask if they knew my family and they would ask me the same question. It was a search that was to go on all over Europe and the world for a very long time.

About three weeks after I had arrived at St. Ottelien, a celebration was held to commemorate the end of the war and our liberation. As part of the celebration, the Jewish Brigade, an auxiliary unit of the British army, came to visit us. When I saw the first Jewish soldiers with the Star of David on their shoulders, I thought that I was imagining things. I could not believe my eyes. It was like seeing a fleet of Flash Gordons—they could not be real. I ran up to them and stroked them to make certain that they were alive. I do not have the words to describe how proud I was. It was more than I had ever dreamed possible. When they mounted the stage to be honored, all of the Nazi propaganda about dirty Jews with two left hands, along with a thousand years of being abused and made fun of, vanished. Poof! There they were—tall, handsome, and Jewish! It was the high point of my young life!

Up until then, I was unsure as to what I should do next. I knew absolutely that I did not want to go back to Poland, but other than that I did not know where to go or what to do. My indecision ended when I saw the Jewish Brigade; on the spot, I decided that wherever they were going, I was going with them. After the celebration, I went up to an officer. Speaking in Hebrew, I begged him to let me go with them, and he said, "Yes." I believe that, at that moment, I was the happiest boy on the planet.

I am convinced that it was the Hebrew that persuaded him to say yes— thank you Dad for insisting that I learn it. But whatever the reason, the next morning with all my possessions—pajamas, pants, shirt, sweater, and a blanket and pillow—I jumped on a truck with the soldiers of the Jewish Brigade and headed out of St. Ottelien. Buoyant with hopes for the future and bursting with a new pride at being Jewish, I was determined to put the past five years behind me. It was not to be. Those years of abuse, hunger, fear, and loss can never be forgotten; they are a part of who I am.

1. Raul Berben, *Dachau, The Official History* (London: the Norfolk Press, 1975), 183. It seems that Ernst Kaltenbrunner, a very high Nazi official, who in April, 1945 was given command of all the German armies in southern Europe, gave orders to the commanders of the Dachau camps to poison all prisoners except "Aryans" from the countries in western Europe.

2. Berben, *Dachau*, 194, describes a number of trains with 2,000 to 3,000 prisoners that were sent south from the Dachau camps between April 23 and 27.

Morris after liberation, wearing the hat of the Jewish Brigade with the Star of David.

Morris and his brother Nachman after they immigrated to the U.S.

Morris and his wife Carol.

Children and Grandchildren of Morris Glass

Henry (Hank): wife, Lynda; daughter, Diana; sons, Alan and Mathew

Charles: wife, Bernice; sons, Brian, Michael, and Jordan

Esta: husband, Dale Gauslin; daughters, Beth and Amy; son, Sean

Richard: wife, Angie; daughters, Eliana and Ava

Robyn: husband, Allen Norrbom; daughter, Molly; sons, Zachary, Gus, and Adam

Michelle: husband, Joshua Blum; daughter, Ella; sons, Sam and Isaiah

Jonathan: wife, Courtney

Brian: wife, Amy; daughters, Natalie and Emmeline; sons, Miles and Michael (wife, Megan)

Bibliography of Selected Works

Adelson, Alan, and Robert Lapides, eds. *Lodz Ghetto: Inside a Community Under Siege*. New York: Penguin Books, 1991.

Aronson, Helen. "Surviving the Holocaust." In *A Time to Share: Powerful Personal Stories for Teaching History and Citizenship*, edited by David Savill, 24-29. London: An Age Exchange Publication, 2002.

Berben, Paul. Dachau, *1933-1945: The Official History*. London: Norfolk Press, 1975.

Berenbaum, Michael and Abraham J. Peck, eds. *The Holocaust and History: The Known, the Unknown, the Disputed and the Reexamined*. Bloomington: Indiana University Press, 1998.

Botwinick, Rita Steinhardt. *A History of the Holocaust, From Ideology to Annihilation*. 3rd ed. Upper Saddle River, NJ: Pearson Prentice Hall, 2004.

Botwinick, Rita Steinhardt, ed. *A Holocaust Reader: From Ideology to Annihilation*. Upper Saddle River, NJ: Pearson Prentice Hall, 1998.

Crowe, David M. *The Holocaust, Roots, History, and Aftermath*. Boulder, CO: Westview Press, 2008.

Dawidowicz, Lucy S. *The War against the Jews, 1933-1945*. New York: Bantam Books, 1986.

Distel, Barbara and Ruth Jakusch, eds. *Concentration Camp Dachau, 1933-1945*. 9th ed. Translated by Jennifer Vernon. Brussels, Belgium: Comité International de Dachau, 1978.

Distel, Barbara and Wolfgang Benz, eds. *Dachau and the Nazi Terror,*
   1933-1945. Dachau: Fuldaer Verlagsanstalt, 2002. (Published for the
   Comité International de Dachau)

Dobroszycki, Lucjan, ed. *The Chronicle of the Lodz Ghetto, 1941-1944.*
   Translated by Richard Lorrie, et al. New Haven, CT: Yale University
   Press, 1984.

Flan, Gila. Singing for Survival: Songs of the Lodz Ghetto, 1940-45.
   Urbana: University of Illinois Press, 1992.

Gross, Jan T. *Neighbors: The Destruction of the Jewish Community in*
   Jedwabne, Poland. New York: The Penguin Group, 2002.

Gutman, Yisrael and Michael Berenbaum, eds. *Anatomy of the Auschwitz*
   Death Camp. Bloomington: Indiana University, 1998.

Hilberg, Raul. *The Destruction of the European Jews.* 3rd ed., Vols.1-3.
   New Haven, CT: Yale University Press, 2003.

Horwitz, Gordon J. *Ghettostadt: Lodz and the Making of a Nazi City.*
   Cambridge, MA: The Belknap Press of Harvard University Press,
   2008.

International Dachau Committee. *The Dachau Concentration Camp, 1933*
   to 1945: Text and Photo Documents from the Exhibition. Dachau:
   Comite´ International de Dachau, 2005.

Kassow, Samuel D. "A Tale of Two Cities." *The New Republic* (May
   6, 2009). Review of Gordon J. Horwitz, Ghettostadt: Lodz and the
   Making of a Nazi City, http://www.tnr.com/article/books/tale-two-cities
   (accessed October 1, 2010).

Luther, Martin. *The Jews and Their Lies.* Los Angeles: Christian
   Nationalist Crusade, 1948.

Preil, Joseph J., ed. *Holocaust Testimonies, European Survivors and*
   American Liberators in New Jersey. New Brunswick, NJ: Rutgers
   University Press, 2001.

Sierakowiak, David. *The Diary of David Sierakowiak: Five Books from the Lodz Ghetto*. Edited by Alan Adelson. Translated by Kamil Turowski. New York: Oxford University Press, 1996.

Trunk, Isaiah. *The Lodz Ghetto, A History*. Translated and edited by Robert Moses Shapiro with an introduction by Israel Gutman. Bloomington: Indiana University Press, 2006.

WEB SITES CONSULTED

United States Holocaust Memorial Museum
www.ushmm.org/
> This is a wonderful site with an abundance of information and resources. *The Holocaust Encyclopedia* is a convenient and excellent reservoir of dates, statistics, maps, photographs, definitions, and other assorted information.

Kaufering.com
http://www.kaufering.com/
> This site was constructed by Joe Kleon, son of James Kleon who was among the American soldiers who liberated Kaufering IV. This was the last camp that Morris was in. It includes maps, numerous photographs, and many other materials about all of the Kaufering camps. It is an amazing site.

Scrapbookpages.com
www.scrapbookpages.com/DachauScrapBook
> This site contains information and pictures about the main camp at Dachau.

We Remember Pabianice!
www.zchor.org/pabianice/pabianice.htm
> This site is devoted to the Jews of Pabianice. It includes population statistics, a map, a picture of the memorial at Chelmno honoring the Jews of Pabianice who were gassed there, and photographs taken during the liquidation of the Pabianice ghetto in 1942.